THE NEW DEAL:
The Historical Debate

PROBLEMS IN AMERICAN HISTORY

EDITOR
LOREN BARITZ
State University of New York, Albany

THE NEW DEAL:
The Historical Debate

EDITED BY
Richard S. Kirkendall
Indiana University

John Wiley & Sons, Inc.
New York • London • Sydney • Toronto

Library of Congress Cataloging in Publication Data:

Kirkendall, Richard Stewart, 1928–   comp.
  The New Deal.

  (Problems in American history)
  CONTENTS: Schlesinger, A. M. Significant but not revolutionary change.—Hacker, L. M. The establishment of state capitalism.—Commager, H. S. The application of accepted and long-familiar principles.—[etc.]
    1. United States—Economic conditions—1933–1945—Addresses, essays, lectures. 2. United States—Economic policy—1933–1945—Addresses, essays, lectures. 3. United States—History—1933–1945—Addresses, essays, lectures. I. Title.

HC106.3.K524   330.9′73′0917   73–4241
ISBN 0-471-48876-3
ISBN 0-471-48877-1 (pbk)

Printed in the United States of America

10 9 8 7 6 5 4 3 2 1

To the Students
of Recent United States History,
University of Missouri–Columbia
1958–1973

SERIES PREFACE

This series is an introduction to the most important problems in the writing and study of American history. Some of these problems have been the subject of debate and argument for a long time, although others only recently have been recognized as controversial. However, in every case, the student will find a vital topic, an understanding of which will deepen his knowledge of social change in America.

The scholars who introduce and edit the books in this series are teaching historians who have written history in the same general area as their individual books. Many of them are leading scholars in their fields, and all have done important work in the collective search for better historical understanding.

Because of the talent and the specialized knowledge of the individual editors, a rigid editorial format has not been imposed on them. For example, some of the editors believe that primary source material is necessary to their subjects. Some believe that their material should be arranged to show conflicting interpretations. Others have decided to use the selected materials as evidence for their own interpretations. The individual editors have been given the freedom to handle their books in the way that their own experience and knowledge indicate is best. The overall result is a series built up from the individual decisions of working scholars in the various fields, rather than one that conforms to a uniform editorial decision.

A common goal (rather than a shared technique) is the bridge of this series. There is always the desire to bring the reader as close to these problems as possible. One result of this objective is an emphasis on the nature and consequences of problems and events, with a deemphasis of the more purely historiographical issues. The goal is to involve the student in the reality of crisis, the inevitability of ambiguity, and the excitement of finding a way through the historical maze.

Above all, this series is designed to show students how experienced historians read and reason. Although health is not contagious, intellectual engagement may be. If we show students something significant in a phrase or a passage that they otherwise may have missed, we will have accomplished part of our objective. When students see something that passed us by, then the process will have been made whole. This active and mutual involvement of editor and reader with a significant human problem will rescue the study of history from the smell and feel of dust.

Loren Baritz

ACKNOWLEDGMENTS

This book is a product of a very large teaching opportunity stretching over fifteen years (1958–1973). It was provided by the University of Missouri–Columbia, and I am very grateful to members of the administration who supported my efforts and to my colleagues in history and in other disciplines who stimulated them. As the dedication suggests, I am especially eager at this time to express my gratitude for the help and encouragement I have received from the students who attended my classes. I am grateful also to an old friend, Loren Baritz, who recruited me for this project, to the people at John Wiley who have been patient as well as very helpful, and to Ida Mae Wolff for her excellent typing. Finally, I wish to thank my wife and my sons for supplying the happy surroundings that seem essential for the historian's work.

Columbia, Missouri   *Richard S. Kirkendall*

ACKNOWLEDGMENTS

CONTENTS

THE NEW DEAL:
The Historical Debate

Introduction

Did the New Deal revolutionize American life? Or was the America that emerged from the 1930's essentially the same as the America of the 1920's? If American life was changed, in what ways was it changed? If it was not changed significantly, why was this so? After all, the American people in the 1930's experienced the most severe economic crisis in their history.

Historians have been debating questions such as these since 1933. They raised them that early because many members of the American historical profession then believed that historians should be concerned with recent developments and contemporary affairs. These particular questions were raised because historians have a peculiar interest in the description, measurement, and explanation of change in human affairs. And questions were raised about the New Deal for it seemed historically important, worthy of the historian's serious attention.

This book seeks to help students think about change in the 1930's. The book's method is historiographical. It traces the development of American historical thought about the New Deal. But the book's aim is historical understanding. While I hope that the reader will become better acquainted with historians and the development of their thought, this is not the major objective of the book. That objective is increased understanding of the New Deal and its impact on American life. The book's basic assumption is that study of the efforts by historians to interpret the New Deal supplies penetrating insights into the New Deal. We shall follow the development of their thought as they brought their particular point of view to bear on Roosevelt's domestic policies and gained new information about them and new perspectives on them.

For most professional historians in the 1930's who were concerned as historians with the New Deal, it seemed a significant part of a long-term development that changed American capitalism and other aspects of American life in desirable ways. This interpretation is developed by Arthur M. Schlesinger in the first selection. He and others called attention to the New Deal's links with the reform movement of the early years of the century. They did see change in the 1930's, but they maintained that it was in line with the hopes, aspirations, and ideas of men such as Theodore Roosevelt and Woodrow Wilson. These historians did not see the New Deal as a radical, revolutionary movement—nor did they desire a revolution. They saw it as evolutionary and reformist. The main result of twentieth-century reform was an enlarged role for government in economic affairs. And since the people exerted a large influence on the government and benefited from its actions, American capitalism became more democratic as a consequence of the success of American reform. The New Deal, in short, reformed and improved capitalism significantly.

If this was the majority view, it was challenged in the 1930's by historians such as Louis M. Hacker, just as Roosevelt and the New Deal were challenged by Norman Thomas and many other critics on the left. There was, in other words, a significant left-wing interpretation of the New Deal in the American historical profession at the time. Although Hacker noted some desirable changes, he did not see the New Deal as democratic. He denied that the New Deal changed America in fundamental and desirable ways and stressed the New Deal's benefits to the nation's most powerful economic groups. Although the role of government was enlarged substantially—and dangerously—the system remained capitalistic. Not a revolution, the New Deal was an effort to revive and prolong the life of a system that had collapsed.

Both of these interpretations survived into the postwar years. Henry Steele Commager, the author of the third selection, devel-

oped an interpretation that resembled Schlesinger's of a decade
earlier, while Broadus Mitchell, the author of the fourth selection, looked at the New Deal from the left as Hacker had in the
1930's. Mitchell, however, represented a point of view that was
losing influence in the profession and in American intellectual
life generally in the postwar years.

The influence of the left was in decline. Once again, surprisingly perhaps, Hacker provides an illustration. He now evaluated
the New Deal from a procapitalist rather than an anticapitalist
point of view and developed an interpretation that emphasized
change rather than continuity. He argued that the New Deal was
a revolution involving a vast enlargement of the role of government in economic affairs.

Some historians of the 1950's who agreed with Hacker about
the amount of change the New Deal produced had greater enthusiasm for the "Third American Revolution." The sixth selection,
by Carl N. Degler, provides the best illustration of this historical
interpretation. Degler stressed several areas in which changes
seemed so great as to justify the label "revolution." They included the development of Big Government and Big Labor.

By the late 1950's and early 1960's, the left was not well represented in the historical profession; neither was the right. In this
situation, a positive appraisal of the New Deal dominated historical interpretation of it. In 1962 Professor Schlesinger polled sev-
enty-five of the profession's most prominent members and
learned that they regarded the leading New Dealer, Franklin
Roosevelt, as one of America's greatest presidents.

Two basic assumptions were involved in the historians' high
regard for Roosevelt and the New Deal. One was that American
history, compared with the history of other nations, was essentially a success story. The other was that one should be "realistic"
in appraising presidents and their programs and should not demand wisdom and success at every point. Influenced by these assumptions, most historians of the New Deal in the early 1960's
believed that it had been quite successful and had improved
American life impressively.

American liberalism exerted a major influence on American
historical thought at the time, and the most prominent liberal
historian, Arthur M. Schlesinger, Jr., developed the largest and

one of the most distinguished histories of the "age of Roosevelt."
Much like his father two decades earlier, the younger Schlesinger
viewed the New Deal as part of the tradition of American reform
that changed America in desirable and democratic ways. The
New Deal represented a superior "middle way" between unfet-
tered capitalism and socialism. It was pragmatic, rejecting the
rigid ideologies, doctrines, and dogmas of both left and right.
The seventh selection provides a small sample of the younger
Schlesinger's work.

By the 1960's, New Deal historiography was developing very
rapidly. Perspective was lengthening, and new sources were be-
coming available. For some time, historians had been able to use
a published edition of Roosevelt's public papers, and other New
Dealers had supplied historians with an unusually large number
of published memoirs, journals, and diaries. In addition, the first
presidential library, the Roosevelt Library at Hyde Park, New
York, which was opened soon after Roosevelt's death in 1945,
supplied a very rich collection of unpublished manuscripts at a
surprisingly early date. These resources stimulated research and
writing on the New Deal, and many specialized studies were
published during the 1950's and 1960's.

As research and publication moved forward, they created especially great difficulties for the argument that the New Deal was
a revolution. The historians did not deny that the New Deal had
changed the system. Some, in fact, such as Irving Bernstein, the
author of the eighth selection, called attention to quite substantial changes. But the new work also emphasized the preparations
for the New Deal. This was, of course, an old theme that had
been developed earlier by the elder Schlesinger and Commager,
among others. But now historians did not merely emphasize the
Progressive movement of the early twentieth century. They also
called attention to the New Deal's debts to World War I and the
1920's. Clarke A. Chambers supplied a major illustration of this
development in a book on social reformers from 1918 to 1933
that demonstrated that progressivism developed during the
1920's and that the developments connected prewar progressivism with the New Deal. He did not deny that the New Deal
changed America significantly, but he suggested that the changes

constituted a stage in a long-term movement and a response to more than the special conditions of the 1930's.

Also, some of the scholars emphasized factors that limited change in the 1930's. Ellis Hawley, the author of the tenth selection, supplied one of the major interpretations of this type. He found defects in the New Deal that were rooted in American culture. The American people and their political representatives could not make up their minds about the ways in which the economic system should be changed, and as a result of their conflict, indecision, and inconsistency, the system was not changed nearly as much nor in the precise ways that different groups of New Dealers desired. One major consequence of this was the survival of Big Business. In spite of the severe depression, it was neither destroyed nor reduced in size.

Other scholars of the 1960's emphasized the strength of right-wing opposition to the New Deal as *the* factor limiting change in the 1930's. Here, James T. Patterson's work was especially important. As the eleventh selection reveals, he stressed the growing strength of a "conservative coalition" in Congress. By the late 1930's, this coalition was effectively resisting the efforts of New Dealers to change American capitalism and other aspects of American life. Because of this effective resistance, the New Deal was not able to change the nation as much as new Dealers desired.

The historians were developing the picture of a New Deal that changed American life but did not revolutionize it. They were supplying evidence on both the predepression conditions and movements out of which the New Deal emerged and on the factors in the 1930's that limited the amount of change that took place during that period.

By the late 1960's, some historians were moving even further away from the revolution thesis. By then, the increasing availability of research materials was not the only major influence on the historical interpretation of the New Deal. Another was the set of obvious problems in American life. Poverty, for example, remained a large part of American life in spite of the reform movement. The problems of American life stimulated the rise of a "New Left" in American politics and in American intellectual life, and this development was reflected in the movement of New Deal historiography. Once again, the New Deal was viewed from the left.

Although the New Left interpretation resembled the work of Hacker and Mitchell in the 1930's and 1940's, it was not a rehash. The new interpretation was heavily influenced by the problems of the present, and its critique of the New Deal was developed much more explicitly and forcefully.

Barton J. Bernstein, the author of the twelfth selection, presented a New Left interpretation of the New Deal. He and his colleagues in the late 1960's not only denied that the New Deal was a revolution but also denied that it changed and improved America significantly. In their view, it had promoted no more than small changes. Rather than stress accomplishments, these historians emphasized shortcomings and failures, especially the New Deal's failure to end the domination of American life by Big Business. Furthermore, in their efforts to explain the failure to produce a desirable social and economic system, Bernstein and others stressed defects in the New Deal itself, especially the ideological weaknesses of the New Dealers. These historians did not point to conservative opposition to the New Deal or to other difficulties in the situation as the explanation of America's failure to undergo a revolution in the 1930's.

The New Left interpretation achieved great prominence but did not sweep the field. Most American historians continued to regard Roosevelt as one of the greatest American presidents, and the New Left interpretation of the New Deal was criticized by historians who penetrated to fundamental assumptions about the ways in which the historical process does work and historians should work.

The critics are represented here by Jerold S. Auerbach, a young historian who emphasized the inadequacies of the New Left historians as historians and the accomplishments of the New Deal. He argued that Bernstein and others were too heavily influenced by the problems and ideas of the present and did not make an adequate effort to understand the 1930's, the aspirations of the people, and the obstacles encountered by those who then hoped to change American life. And Auerbach maintained that in spite of those obstacles and even though the New Deal was not a revolution, it did change American life significantly.

Where are we now after tracing the development of American historical thinking about the New Deal over a period of more than thirty years and examining the debate among historians over the historical significance of the New Deal? We have at least defined the positions in the debate. They include three basic interpretations concerning the amount of change brought about by the New Deal. One labels the New Deal a revolution; the second views it as an important stage in an evolutionary process that had begun long before and insists that though the New Deal produced a significant amount of change it did not produce enough to be called a revolution, and the third denies that the New Deal changed America significantly. The debate also includes two basic appraisals of the New Deal—one negative and one positive. Furthermore, historians have disagreed about the explanations of the changes—or lack of changes—in the 1930's, with some pointing to the New Dealers and others emphasizing other people and other forces.

Perhaps this examination of the record will result in confusion rather than enlightenment. I hope, however, that students will receive intellectual stimulus from the debate among historians. It should force readers to discern and compare the support offered for the different estimates of the amount of change in American life produced by the New Deal and the different explanations of the New Deal's accomplishments or lack of them. The debate should also force students to recognize the influence of assumptions in the work of historians and find ways to make their own appraisals of those assumptions. Change in the amount of evidence available is not the only factor producing change in historical interpretation.

The effort involved in working through this small volume should also provide practical benefits as well as intellectual stimulus. American life of the present day is in part the product of the New Deal. Consequently, an effort to understand it is an effort to understand our present situation. Furthermore, an effort to understand change in the 1930's should help us understand change and the ways of producing it in the 1970's and should assist us in the shaping of our expectations.

1 FROM Arthur M. Schlesinger
Significant But Not Revolutionary Change

Arthur M. Schlesinger was one of the leading American historians of his generation. Born in Xenia, Ohio, in 1888 and educated at Ohio State University and Columbia University, he enjoyed a distinguished academic career at Ohio State, the State University of Iowa, and Harvard University and contributed significantly to the development of American social history as a part of the larger discipline. Prior to his death in 1965, he discussed his career in a memoir, In Retrospect: The History of a Historian, *published in 1963. In it, he recalled that Roosevelt's "threefold program of relief, recovery, and reform had my undeviating approval. Even when liberal friends charged him with moving too slowly or with needlessly yielding ground, I trusted his superb sense of timing and a virtuosity of leadership which knew how to obtain the best results feasible." And he added that he was most impressed with Roosevelt "in his role of public instructor. . . . No previous President . . . had shown so enlightened a conception of the office."*

The following selection was prepared as a supplement to his widely used textbook, Political and Social Growth of the United

SOURCE. Arthur M. Schlesinger, *The New Deal in Action 1933–1938,* New York: The Macmillan Co., 1939, pp. 1–4. Copyright 1939 by the Macmillan Co. Reprinted by permission of Arthur M. Schlesinger, Jr.

States, first published in 1925 and revised in 1933 and 1941 to include recent events. A former student of two pioneers in the study of recent history, James Harvey Robinson and Charles A. Beard, Schlesinger shared a strong conviction in the historical profession of the 1930s that to increase the usefulness of their profession, historians should write about the recent past.

The measures adopted by Congress during its hundred-day special session in the summer of 1933 prefigured the lines along which the New Deal was to develop. Later acts supplemented and modified the methods, but the spirit and purpose and, in large part, the substance of the original legislation remained unchanged. Thrilled by the President's dashing leadership and his swiftness in carrying the program into effect, people felt a stir of new life in the nation and spoke of the "Roosevelt revolution." Thoughtful observers, however, saw in the government's objectives a reassertion of the ideals which the earlier Progressive movement had championed; and in the means devised to attain these ends they perceived an application to the crisis of many of the methods which the Wilson administration had adopted to mobilize the country's economic resources during the World War. It is significant that George W. Norris of Nebraska and "Young Bob" La Follette of Wisconsin, both upholders of the old Progressive ideals, espoused the President's program in Congress, while among those outside Congress who in an official or unofficial capacity helped to give the New Deal form and effectiveness were Bernard M. Baruch, Hugh S. Johnson, and Professor Felix Frankfurter of the Harvard Law School, all of whom had actively participated in the war-time government at Washington in 1917–1918.

If the New Deal seemed a sharp break from the past, a revolution, it was because Roosevelt asserted bold command of the people at the depth of their despair after twelve years of political reaction and governmental drift. In a memorable passage he declared in his inaugural address, "The only thing we have to fear is fear itself—nameless, unreasoning, unjustified terror which paralyzes needed efforts to convert retreat into advance." To this advance he believed the Constitution offered no bar. Just as in the past it had "met every stress of vast expansion of territory, of foreign wars, of bitter internal strife, of world relations," so it would now enable the federal government "to meet extraordinary needs by changes in emphasis and arrangements without loss of essential form. That is why our constitutional system has proved itself the most superbly enduring mechanism the modern world has ever seen."

As the weeks went by, it became unmistakably clear that the New Deal involved no attempt to destroy the capitalist system. Roosevelt and his advisers held to the view that the trouble with capitalism was the capitalists, not the system itself. By extending federal authority over the nation's economic life to a degree unparalleled in American history the President hoped to prevent future abuses of power by financial and industrial interests, to place the business order under firm public control, and to insure the common folk a fuller, freer and securer existence. He acted in the spirit of Macaulay's dictum: "Reform in order to preserve." Because he steered this middle course he was constantly assailed by those to his left who urged him to move faster and farther, and by those to his right who feared he was plunging the country into communism and chaos. But from the plain people, whose mute aspirations he so accurately voiced, he won an ever increasing measure of confidence. They saw the New Deal as America's way of meeting a national crisis that Italy, Russia and Germany had chosen to meet in other and less democratic ways. In particular, the President commanded the warm support of organized labor and of the agrarian groups. These two elements in previous administrations had formed contending interests, but the Roosevelt program, made up in part of their own proposals, betrayed a whole-hearted concern for their joint welfare.

The New Deal involved not only the greatest peace-time centralization of federal authority that the country had ever known, but also a vast extension of the power of the executive at the expense of the legislative. In enacting many of the laws Congress merely laid down broad principles of action, leaving the President free to work out the details, to allocate the funds and oftentimes to set up administrative tribunals as he wished. Soon a multitude of commissions, boards and other agencies sprang up

in Washington, many of them empowered to issue rules and regulations that bore the effect of law though Congress had not ex-
pressly passed upon them. Some of these bodies were limited to
the emergency; others were permanent. Some resembled the Interstate Commerce Commission and the Federal Trade Commission in their powers; others exercised far greater authority. The
public quickly learned to speak of all of them by their alphabeti-
cal abbreviations: NRA for the National Recovery Administration, SEC for the Securities and Exchange Commission, NLRB
for the National Labor Relations Board, and the like.

The setting up of these administrative units caused a rapid expansion of the federal civil service. In four years 241,000 positions were added to the 583,000 already in existence. Of these
new positions three out of every five belonged to the emergency
agencies. Political foes denounced this growth of a "New-Deal
bureaucracy." Protesting against increasing the already burden-
some cost of government, they found further cause for complaint
in the power conferred on many of the new appointees to "in-
trude with official sanction into the private business of citizens."
Since, moreover, the proportion of places outside the merit system was allowed to double in the four years after June, 1932—
rising from one fifth to two fifths of the whole service—they
pointed to the use of many of the offices as political spoils. This
practice they branded as "Farleyism" after the Postmaster-Gen-
eral, the administration's principal dispenser of patronage. New-
Deal supporters defended Roosevelt's apparent indifference to
the examination system of appointment on the ground that the
national emergency called for a recruitment of personnel admit-
ting of no delays, and they took just pride in the fact that no earlier peace-time government at Washington had ever attracted
into the public service, especially the higher ranks, so large a number of disinterested, high-minded and well-trained persons.
Scarcely a college or university in the land failed to contribute
one or more of its faculty for a shorter or longer time to some
branch or other of the new régime.

Facing in 1933 a desperate national crisis, the administration
employed its great powers to accomplish three ends: relief, recovery and reform. The immediate task was to save the fifteen
million unemployed from privation and despair. Beyond this, the

government must help to set the wheels of economic life in motion again. Finally, it undertook certain permanent cures for the deep-seated evils that had produced the industrial breakdown. The business and conservative classes, though friendly to many of the steps for relief and recovery, bitterly fought the proposals for reform. The latter, they argued, if adopted at all, should await normal times. But Roosevelt, eager to make progress while the popular mood permitted, insisted on his full program.

2 FROM   *Louis M. Hacker*
The Establishment of State Capitalism

Somewhat younger than Schlesinger, Louis M. Hacker was one of the leading proponents in the historical profession of the 1930's of a Marxist interpretation of American history. Born in New York City in 1899 and educated at Columbia University, he was a lecturer in economics there in the late 1930's as well as a rather widely read editor and author. He was also one of the founders of the Marxist Quarterly, *a journal published by Marxist intellectuals who were independent of the Communist party. The following selection reflects his brand of Marxism and also his belief that recent history should be written and studied. He hoped to inform Americans of tendencies that alarmed him so that they would take the steps needed to defend themselves "against possible oppression at the hands of the bureaucracy of state capitalism" and to control "this new Leviathan of state capitalism" so that it would be "not our master but our servant." Clearly, he did not share Schlesinger's enthusiasm for the New Deal.*

SOURCE. Louis M. Hacker, *American Problems of Today: A History of the United States Since the World War*, pp. 198–206, 276–281. Copyright 1938. By courtesy of Appleton-Century-Crofts, Educational Division, Meredith Corporation.

Since the New Deal has been described as a revolution, it is important that its real nature be subjected to analysis. The natural history of revolutions in modern times has amply illustrated that they are relatively simple affairs. An economic society, in its youth, is one of very great vigor; not only has its tone been set by a leading class freshly emerged from triumphant struggle, but its purposes have also had the support of nearly all groups in the population. The old vestigial traces have been cut away, class antagonisms—because the opportunities for enterprise in hitherto unexplored regions are so many and so bewildering—have not yet had time to form. The life of the times moves to a new harmony in which what dissonances there are are faint and unimportant.

But as an economic society during the course of its evolution grows into maturity and old age: when the leading problem shifts from expansion into new fields to consolidation of those already won: when for the living energies of men there are substituted institutional patterns—then class lines harden. Revolution sometimes has been employed as a device for the destruction of the constricting molds of such class relations. It wipes them out once and for all and commutes their solidified forms into a new fluidity. The English Revolution, the American Revolution, the French Revolution, the American Civil War, and the Russian Revolution were such virtually clean breaks with the past.

Obviously, in terms of these definitions, the New Deal could scarcely be regarded as revolutionary. Its rationale may be stated in the following group of propositions. The New Deal recognized that the American economy had slowed down and that the forces within it were no longer in equilibrium. Opportunities for capitalist enterprise had contracted: the population had ceased expanding, there were few new great industrial fields to be opened up, oversea markets had been shut off by high tariff walls or were already being closely worked by rival imperialist nations. Business controls had shifted from industrial capitalism to finance capitalism. The spread between capacity to produce and ability to consume was constantly widening. The world market for American agricultural goods had largely disappeared. Not only had new jobs for white-collar and professional workers practically become nonexistent, but there was a surplus rather than a dearth of industrial labor as well. Class lines were being drawn clearly; the danger of class hostilities was no longer remote but already in evidence.

The New Deal, to put it baldly, assumed that it was possible to establish a permanent truce on class antagonisms. The private ownership of the means of production was to continue; but capitalism was to be stopped from exploiting, on the one hand, the producers of its raw materials and, on the other, its labor supply. Agriculture, despite its over-capitalized plant and its growing restriction to the domestic market, was to get a large enough return to allow for the meeting of fixed charges and the purchase of capital and consumer goods. Wage earners were to be assured employment and at least means of subsistence, if not incomes conducive to a decent standard of living. This idea of establishing a balance between American class relations occurred frequently in the writings and utterances of Mr. Roosevelt and his advisers. Thus, as late as March, 5, 1934, the President stated the principle clearly:

"What we seek is balance in our economic system—balance between agriculture and industry and balance between the wage earner, the employer, and the consumer. We seek also balance that our internal markets be kept rich and large, and that our trade with other nations be increased on both sides of the ledger."

The devices employed by the New Deal, for the purpose of revitalizing the American economy, were the following.

First, the restoration of prices. The world-wide collapse that set in with 1930 had been characterized everywhere by a slipping of prices. This phenomenon was nothing new, but the situation took on real aspects of alarm because the great burden of private and public debts (which was new) could not be carried at the same time that prices were falling. According to the Twentieth Century Fund, the long-term debt of American public agencies totaled $33,000,000,000, while that of American corporations and individuals totaled $100,000,000,000. These debts were the real difficulty; to lighten them would have meant repudiation either through wholesale bankruptcy or unchecked inflation, and to avoid this dread alternative the New Deal chose what seemed the easier one of restoring buying power through the raising or the price levels. That the raising of prices was at the heart of the New Deal program and its "definite and determined" policy can be indicated innumerable times from the statements of the New Deal leaders. Thus President Roosevelt, in the speech above cited, said:

"The National Industrial Recovery Act was drawn with the greatest good of the greatest number in mind. Its aim was to increase the buying power of wage earners and farmers so that industry, labor, and the public might benefit through building up the market for farm and factory goods. Employer, wage earner, and consumer groups are all represented on its boards with the government; all three groups with the government must have the interest of all the people as their main responsibility."

At one time or another, the New Deal used the following methods to raise prices: 1. By devaluation of the dollar and an increase in the amount of currency outstanding. 2. By gold purchases from abroad. 3. By seeking to establish parity prices (and also parity income) for agriculture, through corp limitation (with benefit payments) and commodity loans to farmers. 4. By codes of fair competition in industry, to eliminate price cutting.

Second, the revival and expansion of credit. An important characteristic of the crisis had been the slowing down of the movement of short-term and long-term credit into business. The commercial banks, because of their non-liquidity, were not in a position to extend loans for working capital and the purchase of raw materials. The agencies of long-term credit—the savings banks, the insurance companies, trust funds of one kind or another—seeing their earlier investments unproductive, feared to assume further risks until some elements of stabilization had appeared.

The New Deal used the following methods for this purpose: 1. By opening the banks and using the resources of the RFC to achieve liquidity quickly. 2. By putting the control of the open-market policy of the Federal Reserve Banks into the hands of the government itself, so that a public agency now could expand (and contract) credit through open-market operations. 3. By lowering (and raising) the minimum legal reserves required of member banks. 4. By giving the Federal Reserve Board the power to raise (or lower) the margin requirements for security purchases, thus controlling to an extent the amount of bank credit flowing into brokers' loans. 5. By cutting off security affiliates from the control of the commercial banks. 6. By direct loans made by the RFC to business men.

Third, the raising of the purchasing power of the workers. Labor, confronted by shrinking opportunities of employment, was forced to sell its services cheaply and to debase its standards. Sweated industries once more had begun to flourish; child labor had increased; women had resumed homework. To make it possible for the workers to participate once more in the economic life of the nation, the following devices were employed: 1. The establishment of minimum wages and maximum hours in the codes of fair competition. 2. The abolition of child labor in the same codes. 3. The recognition of collective bargaining so that through self-help the same purposes might be achieved. 4. The passage of the Wages and Hours Act of 1938.

Fourth, the reduction of debt. Debt, as had been pointed out, had become onerous. The New Deal sought to come to grips with this problem in two ways, that is to say, by raising prices and by writing down the face value of debt in those places where price change itself could not be entirely and immediately effective. Reduction of debt was to be achieved through the following: 1. In agriculture, the creation of a new fiscal agency (the Federal Farm Mortgage Corporation) which was to make possible the exchange of privately held agricultural long-term paper for semi-public (or public-guaranteed) paper. 2. In the field of home ownership, the creation of a new fiscal agency (the Home Owners Loan Corporation) for a similar purpose. 3. The reform of the federal bankruptcy law to permit private companies and municipalities to come to an understanding with their creditors quickly and at small legal cost. It should be said, here, that in no case was debt reduction thoroughgoing.

Fifth, the revival of foreign trade. Another important characteristic of the crisis was the decline of foreign trade. The New Deal sought to revive American oversea commerce of course; but it was equally interested in the restoration of world trade generally. This dual policy it hoped it could achieve by getting Congress to make the writing of reciprocal trading agreements an executive function. The result was, the State Department was empowered to negotiate commercial treaties whose purpose it was to obtain the lowering of tariff barriers. In the interests of world trade, these agreements were to contain most-favored-nation treatment clauses.

Sixth, the relief of the needy. The crisis had taken a tremendous toll of the American population in undernourishment, illness, invalidism, and psychological maladjustments. The relief of distress was an imminent public duty; and the New Deal came to grips with this hydra-headed problem in the following ways: 1. The lending of money to the states for straight outdoor relief. 2. The creation of a federal agency (the Public Works Administration) which was to lend money to public and quasi-public authorities to finance long-term public construction projects. 3. The writing of social security legislation under which direct federal appropriations and federal matching grants-in-aid were to be made to the states to provide for the unemployables and the permanent needy (the aged, the blind, dependent and crippled children). 4. The provision of employment for the temporary needy, capable to work, in short-term projects financed by the federal government (under the Works Progress Administration).

The above plans were designed to speed recovery. In addition, the New Deal sought to strike at certain evils in the American economy and polity; in other words, it had a reform program. The outstanding reforms that the New Deal was attempting to effect may be listed as follows. (It will be noted that portions of the recovery devices also had reform aspects.) 1. It succeeded in writing legislation and obtaining Supreme Court approval in the interests of labor's rights to organize and bargain collectively under its own leadership. This undoubtedly was the New Deal's outstanding achievement. 2. It passed legislation looking toward the establishment ultimately of adequate unemployment insurance protection. 3. It laid the basis for an old-age annuity fund, under which, in time, all superannuated workers would receive annuities and not doles. 4. It fought for and obtained the establishment of a minimum-wage and maximum-hour code and the abolition of child labor (on a national scale) as humanitarian measures. 5. It recognized the existence of submarginal farmers and tenants who were economially and socially incapable of functioning and it therefore began to experiment with resettlement projects in which such farmers could become productive once more. 6. It set up the Tennessee Valley Authority for the purpose of rehabilitating, economically and socially, the population of the valley and for the purpose of creating an experiment in the public control of electric light and power. This was to serve as a "yardstick" against which the performances of privately controlled power might be measured. 7. It sought to eliminate unnecessary holding company structures in the power field. 8. It set up an agency for the supervision, in the public interest, of security exchanges. 9. It created an agency to guarantee the savings of small depositors in savings and commercial banks. 10. It sought to rehabilitate the permanently depressed bituminous coal industry by establishing an agency to control prices and production. 11. It tired to come to grips with the problem of soil erosion by paying bonuses to farmers to grow soil-conserving crops. 12. It set up a railroad coordinator in an effort to work out a plan for the coordinating and refinancing of the permanently depressed railroad industry. 13. It was preoccupying itself with the question of the rehabilitation of the American merchant marine. 14. It recognized that the building of decent homes was an outstanding social need and it established an agency which, with government financing and subsidies, was to assist quasi-public authorities to create low-cost housing.

It can thus be seen that the New Deal had no intention of overhauling drastically the capitalist system. The mechanism had run down temporarily; it was to be wound up again—after certain repairs had been made and new parts substituted. Having done this, the hope was that there would be suspended in balance and for all time the existing class relations in American society. This was, in brief, an experiment in state capitalism, that is to say, greater government controls over private business and government participation in business directly in those regions where private initiative had definitely failed.

To this extent, therefore, it is possible to characterize the New Deal as being largely a political rather than an economic plan. Its governors did not move over the economic and social scene foot by foot, making adjustments at every point where oppression and injustice had sunk their roots deeply. It operated in those sectors where discontented groups were most effectively organized and whose leadership was most articulate. As a result, the New Deal was able to court successfully the political allegiance of strategically located economic interests; and in this way, therefore, it was able to possess political power.

Thus, in the case of agriculture, the New Deal worked in the interests of the agricultural landlords and commercial farmers almost entirely; and, at that, not all the commercial farmers were assisted. The growers of corn, wheat, and cotton were the most favored; the producers of meat and dairy products and the unorganized growers of vegetables received relatively little support. Landlords having mortgage debts were giving a helping hand; but not tenants whose chief encumbrance was chattel debt. It did next to nothing—its operations were never above the experimental level here—for the great numbers of sharecroppers in the South and the pure subsistence farmers all over the country. It did nothing at all for the more than two million agricultural laborers.

In the case of labor, it worked in the interest of the organized trade unionists; for these, after 1935, had their rights protected by the National Labor Relations Board. But the great mass of the workers of the country were unorganized and had no pressure devices for improving wages and hours and obtaining job security. It was not until 1938 that an hours and wages act was passed to safeguard the industrially underprivileged; and it was still problematical how many persons really could be helped by such legislation.

In the case of business, the New Deal definitely worked in behalf of those interests whose destinies were tied up with foreign trade and investments. It wrote reciprocal trading arreements; it was concerned with the building of a new merchant marine; it sought to safeguard the financial stakes of American investors in those foreign lands where defaults on interest and attempted repudiations of debts were taking place. Notably, its State Department, under Secretary Hull, was adopting an aggressive policy in the Far East for the purpose of protecting the future right of

American capital to exploit this backward economic area. Covertly, the same program was being pushed in Latin America.

Put baldly, the New Deal was a political program in behalf of agricultural landlords and big commercial farmers, organized trade unionists, and oversea investors and imperialist promoters.

It must be apparent, after six years of experimenting, that some of the important evils of the American economy were not attacked at their source. Tinkering with prices was an uncertain device for coming to grips with the heavy burden of capital claims. Demands for fair competition was a Canute like program for checking the onward sweep of monopoly control over prices and production. The problem of excessive saving could not be handled almost entirely through the safeguarding of American rights to invest freely overseas; for this meant imperialist rivalries and the possibilities of war. The taking care of the needy was proper and a humane act. But was it just to demand that the lower middle classes, the workers, and the needy themselves, carry the greater part of the load in the form of heavy concealed taxes on consumption? Such were some of the questions still being asked of the New Deal by more realistic inquirers who wondered what fundamentally had been achieved as the government continued to pile up debt for the purpose of priming the pump of private enterprise.

There was no question that the New Deal had come to grips with a series of important and pressing problems. From the social point of view, it deserved much praise; from the economic, as we have seen, virtually every credit to its favor seemed to produce its own debit. It was in the political sector, however, that the New Deal planning was producing some of the most disquieting elements in the whole program. To provide a rough form of social justice, the New Deal had parted company completely with the nineteenth-century idea of the passive state. It is true that the concept of laissez-faire had never been much more than wishful thinking in any case; indeed, except for England, during the years 1850–1914, the state of the western countries had frequently intervened in economic matters. In the United States, it had espoused protectionism, built the transcontinental railroads out of public funds, turned over the natural resources to favored exploiters. But, taken in the large, the state's intervention had been as a rule in the rôle of umpire among enterprisers. This was all very well as long as capitalism possessed dynamic qualities: for, with opportunities for individual enterprise existing relatively on a wide scale, it was possible for the defenders of the system to talk of *equality* of opportunity. Of course, under capitalism, the notion of equality was a fiction pure and simple: but this fiction was able to sustain the middle class, and the frequent examples of careers from rags to riches, so to speak, gave political authority the justification it required for refusing to come to the assistance of the victims of economic and class oppression.

The depression of 1930 and its continuance indicated clearly enough that capitalist progress had slowed up, if it had not ceased altogether. Now, the state's function changed—virtually over night. Its part as umpire was magnified and extended into other regions—as in the case of the establishment of the National Labor Relations Board and the old-age reserve fund and unemployment insurance fund. Its social service functions were expanded, particularly as regards the handling of the problems of the unemployed, the unemployables, and other forms of dependency. More significant, in terms of the basic nature of the state, it began to initiate projects and enterprises of an economic character. The state, in other words, was beginning to take on the essential color in many domains of private enterprise. It was borrowing money, of course; but it had always done this, although heretofore this had been merely for the maintenance of the civil establishments of government and military defense. This time, however, it was borrowing money for the purposes of buying and selling commodities, processing goods, creating electric power and light, dealing in real estate, engaging in warehousing, the banking business, the operation of ships and railroads, and the like. And it was using the organizational forms of private enterprise: corporations and corporate agencies which possessed assets of their own, reported earned income, had great rolls of employees, some of them running into the thousands—and a few of which, like private business itself, were chartered under the laws of Delaware, Maryland, and other jurisdictions.

This was transformation. The state no longer pretended to be the laissez-faire, or passive, state: it was now the capitalist state.

We were beginning to live under the authority of state capitalism. In short, the general theory and functions of capitalism remained: private ownership of the means of production, unhampered individual accumulation, the wage system, inequality of income based upon property possession and not social need, a class society. In some areas, however, the state was beginning to act as enterpriser; and in a few, indeed, as a monopolist enterpriser as in the case of the TVA.

This state of affairs, obviously, raised a number of important questions.

1. Was it possible to dismantle the capitalist state and restore it to its original passive rôle? A demand for such a return came from the New Deal critics on the right. They argued that state interference, control, and initiation were hampering and burdening with excessive taxes private enterprise, and the fear of an overweening public authority was preventing the movement of fresh capital into new undertakings. But the return to so-called rugged individualism, it was more and more plain, was out of the question. Rugged individualism left in its train too many casualties: the permanently disemployed, gross inequalities of income, marginal and submarginal producers. With the international division of labor at an end and fewer and fewer opportunities for fresh imperialist adventure existing, the modern capitalist world was confronted by excess productive capacity and excess savings. State intervention was necessary, from the viewpoint of capitalism itself, to prevent social unrest if not profound dislocations.

2. Was state capitalism leading to socialism or communism? This also was problematical. State capitalism was not destroying old class relations: it was simply freezing them. Where the state was expropriating property actually or in effect (as in the case of private utility companies competing with the TVA or private insurance companies holding farm mortgage paper), it was compensating: a rentier class therefore was being substituted more and more for an enterpriser class. Nor were the underprivileged being provided for in terms of their social necessities and their full individual potentialities. The wage system was being maintained: it scarcely mattered who was employer, whether it was government or private business. It should also be pointed out

that this New Deal state was initiating projects as a rule in those realms where private capitalism had failed. This left a large region of enterprise—by far the greater part—for private ownership and private accumulation.

3. Was the capitalist state a responsive state? It was at this point that one's judgments could be regarded as quite certain. Plainly, the New Deal state was not a responsible authority. It is true, the social agencies—NLRB, WPA, FERA, Social Security Board—were being scrutinized closely: by Congress, the press, independent popular agencies. This was all to the good; for this was one of the ways a democracy functioned and in this way public authority was held responsible. But the same could not be said of the great majority of the corporate agencies, that is to say, these federal corporations which were in business. The pattern was too complex and too obscure for popular control. These agencies came and went, often without hails or farewells. They were created by Congress, sometimes only by implication; by Presidential orders; by intra-departmental memoranda. Often they were run, presumably, by Cabinet officers who, in the nature of things, were compelled to delegate powers to anonymous lesser officials. Frequently, there existed interlocking directorates, so that there was being built up a concentrated financial (and political) power in the hands of a few individuals. The accounts of these agencies were not uniform. Sometimes they reported to the General Accounting Office, sometimes they did not. In some cases, even, annual reports were never drawn up to become public documents. Nevertheless, these agencies were using public funds, borrowing and lending among each other, and beginning and terminating various kinds of businesses.

Where was the danger? Without responsiveness, such a state was likely to develop a bureaucracy with its own institutional safeguards and rhythms of being. For its maintenance (as well, of course, for the carrying out of the programs it was supporting) the productive energies of the nation would have to be dipped into more and more. In short, under state capitalism—as under merchantilism in the seventeenth and eighteenth centuries and under modern-day fascism and, perhaps, too, Soviet-style communism—a constant hemorrhage of capital would be required to maintain an apparatus which, to the bureaucrat, was more important than anything else.

It was a political axiom that authority without responsibility led to tyranny. It was beside the point whether the tyranny was that of an absolute monarchy, an oligarchy, a party, or a bureaucracy. The New Deal was in process of developing such a bureaucracy, whose allegiance was almost entirely to the Executive, only in slight measure to the Legislature and the popular will. In a period of stress and under cover of an emergency, the Executive always can succeed in arrogating to itself extraordinary powers. This had happened during our Civil War and World War; but following them, these powers of the Executive had been terminated. But what of a permanent emergency, if the paradox may be permitted? For the New Deal was pleading the existence of an emergency for whose conclusion it was holding out no immediate hopes. The Executive's powers, therefore, were constantly being expanded, the agencies increased, the lesser and anonymous officials and directors multiplied, and the public pay roll enormously distended.

What was needed, as has been said, was responsibility, so that the democratic processes could be maintained in fluid form. The following desiderata constituted a minimum program for present-day America, notably as regards the federal corporations: (1) reporting to Congress and the General Accounting Office; (2) uniformity of accounting practice; (3) complete control over interlocking directorates. So much government could do. The responsibility of the public was even greater. It was imperative that popular agencies be set up to scrutinize and criticize the activities of the new agencies and call officers who were overreaching themselves to account. The defense of democracy was the task not only of the Executive but of the Legislature and the people as well. For democracy could be imperiled not only from without but also from within.

3 FROM　　　　*Henry Steele Commager*
The Application of Accepted and Long-Familiar Principles

Henry Steele Commager was close to Hacker chronologically and geographically but much closer to Schlesinger intellectually. Born in Pittsburgh three years after Hacker was born in New York City, Commager witnessed the developments of the 1930's from a New York vantage point, teaching in New York University after receiving a Ph.D. from the University of Chicago and before moving uptown to Columbia University. A disciple of Vernon Parrington, who was a pioneer in the study of American intellectual history and one of the giants of the "Progressive School" of American historiography, Commager emphasized intellectual continuity in his interpretation of the New Deal. The New Dealers, he said, in effect, changed American capitalism in ways that the Populists and Progressives had tried to change it. The results, while not revolutionary, were significant and desirable.

The decade of the nineties is the watershed of American history. As with all watersheds the topography is blurred, but in the perspective of half a century the grand outlines emerge clearly. On the one side lies an America predominantly agricultural; concerned with domestic problems; conforming, intellectually at least, to the political, economic, and moral principles inherited from the seventeenth and eighteenth centuries—an America still in the making, physically and socially; an America on the whole self-confident, self-contained, self-reliant, and conscious of

SOURCE. Henry Steele Commager, *The American Mind: An Interpretation of American Thought and Character Since the 1880's,* New Haven: Yale University Press, 1950, pp. 41, 54, 337, 338, 352–353. Copyright 1950 by Yale University Press. Reprinted by permission of the publisher.

its unique character and of a unique destiny. On the other side lies the modern America, predominantly urban and industrial; inextricably involved in world economy and politics; troubled with the problems that had long been thought peculiar to the Old World; experiencing profound changes in population, social institutions, economy, and technology; and trying to accommodate its traditional institutions and habits of thought to conditions new and in part alien.

The great issues of the nineties still commanded popular attention half a century later; the seminal minds of that decade still directed popular thought. Problems of isolation and internationalism, of laissez faire and government planning, of the causes and cures of panics, the contrasts of progress and poverty, the humanizing of urban life, the control of business and the rights of labor, the place of the Negro and the immigrant in society, the improvement of agriculture and the conservation of natural resources, the actualization of democracy into social security—all these things which had monopolized public interest in the nineties, seemed no less urgent in the 1930's and 1940's. The roots of the New Deal were in populism, the origins of world power in the Spanish War and the acquisition of Hawaii and the Philippines. Fifty years after their formulation the American was still exploring the economic ideas of Veblen, developing the sociological doctrines of Lester Ward, elaborating on the historical theories of Henry Adams and the historical interpretations of Frederick Jackson Turner, experimenting with the educational theories of John Dewey, amplifying the philosophy of William James, applying the artistic standards of Louis Sullivan and Thomas Eakins, accommodating political institutions to the teachings of Frank Goodnow and Woodrow Wilson, catching up with the juridical doctrines of Justice Holmes. Notwithstanding two world wars, enormous material growth, astonishing advances in technology, and revolutionary changes in science, the threescore years that came after 1890 possessed an unequivocal unity.

Notwithstanding irrelevant differences in party allegiance, superficial differences in political methods, and deep differences in character, these five great leaders of American democracy in the twentieth century, Bryan, LaFollette, Wilson, Theodore and Franklin Roosevelt, had much in common. All were children of the Enlightenment, as it were, inspired by new insights and equipped with new tools. All were evolutionists—even Bryan, for all his religious fundamentalism. All were pragmatists, more concerned with the machinery of government than with its façade. All recognized, though with verying degrees of perception, the economic bases of politics and the role of pressure groups in the formulation of policy. All understood the nature of public opinion and how to inspire and to guide it.

The most illuminating test of their conversion to the evolutionary and pragmatic philosophy was their attitude toward that symbol of traditionalism, the judiciary. As they looked upon the Constitution as a tool rather than a symbol, so they regarded the Court not as a Delphic oracle but as a political institution. Bryan campaigned in 1896 against the judicial nullification of the income tax—which he had helped write—and the use of the injunction in labor disputes. Roosevelt, who demounced him for this heresy, came himself to advocate the recall of judicial decisions, and for his own heresy forfeited the support of stalwarts like Henry Cabot Lodge and Elihu Root. LaFollette, who saw the courts frustrate public policy for a quarter-century, ran for the presidency on a platform that branded judicial conduct a "plain violation of the Constitution." Wilson, who never faced a judicial crisis—except perhaps in that impudent nullification of the Child Labor Law which remains one of the scandals of American constitutional history—confessed his position boldly enough by his appointment to the Supreme Court of the greatest of sociological jurisprudents, Louis Brandeis, and of the liberal John H. Clarke. And Franklin Roosevelt's response to the attempt of the judiciary to fasten a strait jacket about the government took the form of the boldest program for judicial reform that had ever been attempted by an American president.

What populism and progressivism, the New Freedom and the New Deal, meant in terms of political philosophy was the final repudiation of laissez faire and the explicit recognition of government as a social welfare agency. What it meant in terms of constitutional theory was the unqualified triumph of the doctrine of board construction. The pernicious notion that there was some inevitable conflict between man and the state had long embarrassed American politics. Distrust of government, inherited from the Revolutionary era, approved by Jefferson, endowed with perverse rationalization by Herbert Spencer, gave way at last to the realization that the government was man organized politically, and that vigilance—still the price of liberty—was not synonymous with paralysis. The "necessary evil" of Thomas Paine had become so necessary that it was no longer an evil.

The task that confronted Franklin Roosevelt when he came to the presidency in the dark days of the spring of 1933 was one that taxed statesmanship to the utmost. But it was, or appeared to be, practical rather than philosophical. The contributions of Bryan and Roosevelt, LaFollette and Wilson, were a matter of history, and in intelligent circles the principles which they had so ably espoused had ceased to be controversial. No student of politics, outside the judiciary, questioned the propriety of the evolutionary interpretation of the Constitution or of the application of pragmatic methods to administration, and Wilson's successors, by turning the government itself over to business, admitted not only the importance but the priority of economic considerations. Roosevelt's task, therefore, was not to formulate new principles but to apply those already accepted and long familiar.

4   FROM   *Broadus Mitchell*
Intellectual Confusion and Economic Failure

Closer to Schlesinger in age and point of origin, Broadus Mitchell was closer to Hacker in point of view. Born in Georgetown, Kentucky in 1892, Mitchell was educated at the University of South Carolina and Johns Hopkins University. Although he was a teacher and a publishing scholar, he was also an "activist," participating in such organizations as the Urban League, the League for Industrial Democracy, and the Socialist party. While

SOURCE. Broadus Mitchell, *Depression Decade: From New Era Through New Deal 1929–1941*, New York: Rinehart & Co., Inc., 1947, pp. 365–369, 405–407. Copyright, 1947, by Broadus Mitchell. Reprinted by permission of Holt, Rinehart and Winston, Inc.

*preparing the book from which the following selections were tak-
en, a book that was part of a multivolume series on the economic
history of the United States, he also served as an economist for
the International Ladies Garment Workers Union. Although he
believed that the New Deal produced some changes, including
some desirable ones, he devoted much of his attention to deficiencies and failures and obviously assumed that much more
should and could have been accomplished.*

Reviewing the whole performance from 1933 to the outbreak
of war in Europe in 1939, we find that the New Deal took full
advantage of the President's promise, early given, that efforts
were experimental, that if one expedient proved faulty, another
would be tried. The New Deal was grandly opportunist. The
term might be used as a condemnation, but is here employed as
a description. The administration did not stop at change of emphasis, but resorted to reversal of plans. Attempted inflation was
abandoned for policing of prices. Profuse government spending
was followed by restriction and spending again. Business collu-
sion was at first promoted, later prosecuted. Economic nationalism was embraced, then rejected. These were the conspicuous
about-faces; minor vacillations need not be mentioned.

Holding to the intention of rehabilitating the accepted economic system—call it capitalist, private profit, individual enterprise, what you will—the New Deal twisted and turned to shake
off the burden of mass unemployment. Success in this was
bound to be the test of validity. Failure was especially vexing because the goal seemed near with the economic improvement of
1937, only to recede with the fresh slump later in that year
which continued into 1938. "Recession" it was called instead of
"confirmed depression," but the softer word did not cure the dis-
crediting fact. Lost ground was painfully regained, but the country did not see its way out of the woods until the advent of World
War II.

Despite all efforts—Hoover's orthodoxy tempered with boldness, and Roosevelt's boldness mixed with orthodoxy—the nation did not emerge from the decade of depression until pulled

out by war orders from abroad and the defense program at home. The rescue was timely and sweet, and deserved to be made as sure as possible. Whether the involvement of the United States in the war through progressive departure from neutrality was prompted partly by the reflection that other means of extrication from economic trouble had disappointed, nobody can say. No proponent did say so. Instead, advocates of "all-out aid to Britain," convoying of Allied shipping, and lend-lease took high ground of patriotism and protection of civilization. History may see a causal connection, conscious or not, between dull times and democracy vindicated.

Roosevelt, called upon to lead just when the banking crisis had rapidly matured, lacked plans but possessed what was of greater immediate importance—a superb purpose. Confident of his own powers, he poured strength into the people. His inaugural assurance was a moral triumph, outweighing in influence the legislative improvisations of the next "hundred days." Someone has said that economic law is what a country decides it wants. The aphorism was illustrated then. Hearts beat again, minds went to work. There was a grandeur in the promise, albeit not always borne out in the performance.

Roosevelt's course falls, roughly, into four stages:

1. Intimate government participation in banking, currency management, industry, and agriculture. Erring bankers were reproached; the currency was cut loose from gold and controlled for national ends; industry and labor, through NRA, were drawn into a partnership with government which had collusive as well as merely cooperative features; staple crops were restricted when the AAA paid farmers not to produce. Other projects were included, such as more generous federal relief through CWA, FERA, and WPA. This effort, or combination of efforts, came to an end with the Banking Act of 1935 and the revolt of the Supreme Court when it invalidated NRA and AAA. The President's stigmatic "horse and buggy" outburst and his thwarted attempt suddenly to change the composition of the Court were expressions of disappointment followed by a change of tack.

2. The next stage, 1935–1937, took the wind on a new quarter, but the sails of government were to be filled by the same breeze of higher prices at all costs. The NRA was a wreck and

had to be abandoned, but the AAA was patched up and still served its turn, while fiscal freedom had been happily vouchsafed by liberal Supreme Court decisions covering currency powers. Though government was no longer allowed to be the partner of business, it could and must be the patron of business. The method was to support private enterprise, even superseding it where necessary, through robust spending and lending. This was the period of "pump priming," as it was fondly called, the instruments being RFC subventions, and vast public works including TVA and public housing.

This was the high tide of the New Deal in its recovery rather than its reform phase. Perhaps the administration lacked the courage of its convictions. Maybe the doubts which it developed were the results of the cries of those alarmed over deficits. More likely the New Dealers concluded from the gratifying business indexes that the spend-lend pump priming had turned the trick, that the depression was conquered, and that therefore the government could resign its efforts. Whatever be the case, expectations were premature. The "recession" or relapse of the autumn of 1937 was bitterly disappointing to New Dealers and, in the eyes of the critics, discredited the policies used.

3. The President and his strategists, never committed to consistency, recovered poise faster than did the country. Refusing to resume their price-raising program, or to deprecate it as having been a mistaken policy on their part, they pretended innocence of the error, and sent up the hue and cry after the culprits, now designated as private concentrations of economic power which deserved to be exposed and prosecuted. One miscreant had donned tunic and badge of policeman, and pointed to the others —monopolies and all their cohorts—as the public enemies. This was the New Deal's nimblest shift of role. The solemn investigation by the Temporary National Economic Committee into the evil lapse of competition was the sequel. This third policy of the New Deal in attacking the depression was at length abandoned in mingled minor chagrin and major relief of mind.

4. The passing embarrassment was caused by the fact that chief inquisitors into the wickedness of price and production control scampered from the committee hearings to assume command of OPA and Emergency Management. And a vast anxiety

was overcome because to the benefits of the "arsenal of democracy" had been added America's full engagement in World War II.

What were the relative advantages offered by the New Deal to various interests in the American economy? We may answer the question with rough accuracy. Agricultural proprietors conceded least for what they received. Banks and other financial institutions came off next best as beneficiaries. Industry and commerce, embraced in NRA, were third; they granted labor's right to collective bargaining, agreed to minimum wages and maximum hours, and got in return suspension of the antitrust acts, or "industrial self-government."

Labor received guarantees which were more important for the future than at once. Unequivocal establishment in law of the right of organization and independent collective bargaining offered opportunity of which labor availed itself. The Fair Labor Standards Act set national minimum wages and maximum hours which were to be improved upon. In addition to legal sanctions, the New Deal gave organized labor strong moral encouragement which helped launch it on a larger career in the economy. Still, anti-injunction legislation had already, before NRA, gone far to establish the freedom of independent unions; shorter hours of the individual worker and the throwing out of child labor were no great inconvenience in a period of huge labor surplus, while higher hourly wages had long been urged by enlightened employers as a means of ensuring profits and industrial stability. Further, though the President begged that prices should not be raised until some time after wages had been increased, this was never more than a pious hope. Industry held out its hands to have bonds of stout rope taken off, and to accept in return wrappings of packthread.

At the outset, labor fared not so well as employers. In order to benefit by government liberality, a sector of the economy must be tolerably organized to deal with its problems with or without public assistance. "To him that hath shall be given. . . ." Producers of the great farm staples had their associations which, despite disappointment in previous legislative attempts, continued vigorous lobbying; the masses of small farmers, though they took no part in the work of the Grange or the Farm Bureau Federation, were accustomed to being corralled by government farm agents scattered through every locality. Banks, as compared with the other groups here discussed, were few in number, interdependent, organized officially and unofficially, and enjoyed the solicitude not only of the Secretary of the Treasury but of every counselor of the President, for all parts of economic society were felt to hang on an able banking system. Considering the distress of the banks, it is a question whether they did not get even more than the farmers. The best assets, surrendered to the Reconstruction Finance Corporation in return for cash elsewhere unobtainable, were frozen so long as the banks remained closed, and would have shrunk to a fraction of their value had the banks dared reopen except according to government plan with government support.

Industry had the benefit not only of such over-all organizations as the Chamber of Commerce of the United States and the National Association of Manufacturers and their local divisions, but of a thousand trade associations which had at least escaped, if not the notice, the effective hostility, of the Federal Trade Commission, and antitrust prosecution. The concentration of control in industry was equally or more important in facilitating united action, since the habit of following leaders spread influence beyond the bailiwick of absolute authority. Besides, if depression had eliminated weak units of industry and commerce, it left the remaining stronger ones in a better position.

In contrast, organized labor had never numbered more than 10 per cent of American workers, had suffered losses of membership in the prosperous twenties, and was critically weakened by three years of depression and unemployment. The masses of workers had been no more than touched by organization, and when, in millions, they lost their jobs, instead of improving the case of those still drawing wages, the unemployed were a constant threat to standards of hours and pay and to unionism.

Thus we may venture the summary that farmers and bankers came into the New Deal as preferred claimants; industry obtained the opportunity, in return for certain concessions to labor, to do openly what it had already been doing secretly; while labor must first organize to lay hold on what was offered it, and needed all of the defense that the National Labor Board and the National Labor Relations Board could give it, and more. We have not considered here the remaining distinguishable economic interest. What was the *quid pro quo* of consumers? Being least organized, consumers were least capable in the grand bargaining, if indeed, it may be said that consumers could bargain at all. The higher prices and the reduced output, which were to be the main means to recovery, must fall on their devoted heads, with only the assurance that whatever started the economy going again must benefit the buyers of goods and services, and that, after all, consumers were inextricably confused with all elements receiving direct advantages. If labor was little consulted by NRA, consumers were present only by proxy. However, *pro forma* recognition was progress, and doubtless prepared the way for more serious wartime protection, as in the Office of Price Administration.

The New Deal failed, if we judge by its ability to bring about a fully functioning economy, for at the end of six years of effort the nation still had some 10,000,000 unemployed. The New Deal reduced unemployment, both absolutely and relatively, as compared with what it had been when the administration took office in the spring of 1933. But the 10,000,000 remained as a stubborn reproach. A companion purpose had been to increase the measure of social justice. Success in this would necessarily be slower, and the means of gauging achievement are less definite. It is not surprising that President Roosevelt, midway in his reform program, was obliged to describe one third of the nation as ill fed, ill clothed, ill housed. Nor should one expect this condition to be removed in another three years; perhaps thirty years would not be too long an interval to allow for such a widespread renovation. To produce something like social justice, much preliminary work had to be done that would not show quick or concrete results. The situation of those worst off had been ameliorated, and glaring abuses had been more or less corrected. The unemployed had relief, direct or through public works, and half the labor population had some guarantees in the new social insurance. The farmers' plight had been notably lessened, hard-pressed homeowners had been assisted or rescued, here and there slum spots had been cleared. Looseness of banks, deceptions of financial promotion, and harmful conduct of holding companies had been rebuked and restrained, while labor unions were recognized in law and in practice.

However, these tangible accomplishments, excellent in themselves, were not as significant as the hope, indeed self-confidence, which the New Deal had aroused in the nation. The New Deal proclaimed, and went a distance to prove, that we need not be frustrated by inscrutable misfortune, but could be masters of our future. This mental candor and moral lift formed the true contribution, and for them all praise is due.

5   FROM   *Louis M. Hacker*
The Third American Revolution

By 1957, both Louis Hacker and the national and international situations had changed significantly since 1938. He had moved up in the academic world, having become a professor at Columbia in 1948 and a dean of its School of General Studies in 1952, and the situation had moved from depression to prosperity and from threat of war with Germany and Japan to Cold War with Communist nations. Hacker's attitude toward capitalism had changed from negative to positive, while his appraisal of Marxism had moved in the opposite direction, and he had become critical of "The Anti-Capitalist Bias of American Historians," a criticism that he expressed with characteristic vigor in Capitalism and the Historians, *a book edited by F. A. Hayek in 1954.*

Hacker's interpretation of the New Deal had changed substantially. He no longer denied that it was a revolution. In fact, he now insisted that it was. And he did so even though he continued to maintain that it had not rejected capitalism. The changes in the economic activities of government seemed to him to consti-

SOURCE. Louis M. Hacker, *American Capitalism: Its Promise and Accomplishment*, Princeton: D. Van Nostrand Company, Inc., pp. 78–87. Copyright © 1957 by Louis M. Hacker. Reprinted by permission of Van Nostrand-Reinhold Company.

tute a revolution. Also, his appraisal of the New Deal was more favorable. He found defects in it that limited capitalism's success in the 1930's, but he believed that it strengthened and improved the economic system.

REVOLUTIONS IN AMERICAN HISTORY

There have been three great turning points in the American economy and these have notably occurred as a result of positive action by government. The first stemmed from the adoption of the Hamiltonian program (1791–1795), the second from that of the Republican party program (1861–1865), and the third from that of the New Deal (1933–1939). In every instance, responsibilities assumed by government toward business—in directing, supporting, even subsidizing—gave a new direction to enterprise and started it off on hitherto unexplored paths.

The Hamiltonian program put its emphasis on finance: the integrity of public and private credit would encourage accumulation and the investment functions in America by both domestic and foreign risk-takers; at the same time, it was willing to participate, as in the federal government's purchase of a part of the stock of the First Bank. The Republican program sought to encourage industrialization and the expansion and diversification of the domestic market: by high tariffs, large-scale railroad construction, easy land and immigration policies. It, too, was ready to participate, as in the case of the subsidizing of many of the trunk railroads through land grants and loans.

THE NEW DEAL AS REVOLUTION

The New Deal went further than its two predecessors: for not only did it regulate and direct, but it also put government into business. Following the adoption of the Hamiltonian and Republican party programs, a great burst of new energy and enterprise occurred, indeed, whole companies of new innovators made their appearance. Fresh avenues for investment were explored, opportunities for employment were opened up, new fortunes appeared: economic change and economic progress went hand in hand. The New Deal's contribution, perforce, was different. The country was confronted by collapse; revival was the prime necessity of the time; and every sort of expedient—if not plan—restorted to to put men back to work and to start the wheels of industry revolving once more.

A new enterpriser now appeared, the government functionary who headed a public corporation which could buy and sell, lend and borrow, produce and distribute; and this obviously was intervention of an entirely different order. In time, the directors of the New Deal referred to their activities as the "Welfare State": its purpose was as much to assure security as it was to promote economic progress. And the chief method? It was that of "deficit financing": government expeditures, by making possible the resumption of the normal industrial processes, would encourage private enterprise to take up the burden of advance. Only in part did this tactic succeed, for private companies were slow in following government's lead. Indeed, it was not until 1940—and in the midst of war preparations—that the economy began to leap ahead, increasing employment, capital formation, real income.

Nevertheless, a revolution had occurred and it was one that turned out to be permanent. It was this: government was assuming responsibility for the security and welfare of its working populations and for the stability of the whole economy. High employment, from thence on, was to be a concern of government; so was social security as regards old age and dependency; agriculture was to be protected against the mischances of the market; saving deposits were to be guaranteed. Even more profoundly, government accepted responsibility in these areas: it was to use its great weight to prevent too sharp swings in the business cycle (by monetary and fiscal controls, public-works planning and outlays) ; and it was to help in a more equitable distribution of the annual national product (by maintaining high real wages and by taxation) . Here, in this last, the great lesson of the depression had been learned: the economy, associated with private enterprise, could endure and grow only if the purchasing power of its own producers was maintained at high levels.

NEW DEAL ANALYSIS OF THE ECONOMY

The New Deal planners and managers operated upon certain theoretical assumptions: some were true, some false; some were maintained up to the end, and some were quickly abandoned.

1. It was assumed that, in many areas, capital plant had been overexpanded; it was imperative, in consequence, to limit new investment and production. This was true of agriculture, petroleum, and coal, and special authorities in each instance were set up to control production. The same idea was extended to all industry under the short-lived National Recovery Act of 1933–1935, under which many industries, in the process of self-policing by the writing of "codes," were permitted to supervise the use of existing plant and new-plant expansion. John Maynard Keynes' ideas concerning limiting opportunities for investment (the existence already of a so-called "mature economy") were accepted by many New Deal economists; they looked, therefore, to social investment by government rather than to private investment by companies for the revival and rejuvenation of the economy.

2. Prices were being "managed," or they were "sticky" in important areas of enterprise, notably among the heavy-goods industries. This was due to imperfect competition; a frontal attack on monopoly practices was in order to reduce such rigidities.

3. Labor's position in the economy was an unequal one. Higher incomes would restore purchasing power; recognition of trade unions and collective bargaining would create checks on management vis-à-vis profits. Government also was to guarantee a minimum wage and maximum hours of work.

4. Debt burdens—notably onerous as prices continued to fall —had to be lightened. This was true of agriculture, municipalities, many industrial companies, privately owned homes.

5. The public-utilities industry was managed by holding companies on the one hand and was incapable of financing large-scale programs of new power installations on the other. Holding companies were to be dissolved; government was to help (particularly in rural areas) the financing of power transmission and the purchase of appliances; a great program of expansion in the

Tennessee Valley was to be undertaken by a public corporation, the TVA.

6. Social security—against unemployment, old age, dependency—was a legitimate interest of government.

7. There were dark areas in cities and the countryside that required public concern: low-cost housing had to be built to help in the battle against the slums; marginal and submarginal farmers had to be helped; youth had to be put to work—on conservation projects if nothing else offered.

8. The whole banking system needed overhauling. Commercial banking had to be taken out of the investment banking business; the investor needed protection through supervision over houses issuing securities and the securities markets. Notably, central-banking needed strengthening to give government greater controls over the monetary and fiscal mechanisms.

9. The United States had to return to the world market on a sound footing. Freer trade had to be restored, at the same time that an orderly movement of American surpluses of cotton, cereals, tobacco, oil, and copper into foreign markets was devised.

TACTICS OF THE NEW DEAL

The programs of the New Deal planners, flowing from the above analysis, were pursued along the following lines:

1. Prices were to be restored and maintained. To accomplish this, the dollar was devalued; gold and silver were purchased from abroad; limitations on the production of agricultural products, petroleum, and coal were imposed; industrial "codes of fair competition" (under the NIRA) were permitted to fix prices. In the case of agriculture, crop loans and subsidies were also required to make production control work.

2. Debt was to be reduced. The problem of debt was to be handled by price rise and by writing down debt. For agriculture, a public corporation, the Federal Farm Mortgage Corporation, made possible the exchange of privately held farm mortgages for semipublic (or public-guaranteed) mortgages. The Home Owners' Loan Corporation permitted the same kind of conversion in

the case of residential mortgages. Bankruptcy laws were rewritten to give relief to businesses and municipalities.

4. Credit was to be revived and expanded. The Reconstruction Finance Corporation (created in 1932) was given large sums and vast powers to make loans to public bodies and private businesses. Virtual public control over the Federal Reserve System was established so that the expansion (and contraction) of credit would now be a concern of government. The Board of Governors of the Federal Reserve System now had the power to lower (and raise) the legal reserve requirements of banks and the right to raise (or lower) the margin requirements for the purchase of securities. As the New Deal resorted increasingly to deficit financing, with public securities flowing into banks, it was ready to accept the thought that the monetization of debt would take place and thus the way would be eased for the expansion of business credit.

5. Labor's purchasing power was to be raised. First in the codes written under the NIRA and then through the Fair Labor Standards Act of 1938, minimum wages and maximum hours were fixed and child labor was abolished. It was assumed that with the recognition of trade unions and the acceptance of collective bargaining, organized labor would be able to raise its own standards. The National (Wagner) Labor Relations Act of 1935 compelled bargaining with unions, once they had been established by election as the workers' representatives, but it also outlawed so-called unfair practices on the part of management.

6. Social security—against unemployment, invalidity, old age, dependency—was a responsibility of government. Many government agencies—Works Progress Administration, Public Works Administration, Civilian Conservation Corps—were set up to create jobs or induce public bodies, by loans, to embark on programs of public works. Unemployables were to be taken care of by local authorities, with financial assistance from the federal government. Funds were established to provide for the unemployed and the aged after retirement.

7. New homes were to be built with the help of federal subsidies.

8. The investor and saver were to be protected. The Securities

and Exchange Commission was given wide authority over new corporate security issues and the activities of security exchanges. The Federal Deposit Insurance Corporation was set up to guarantee savings deposits in banks up to $5,000 (later raised to $10,000).

9. The electric power and light industry was to be brought under closer public control. The Tennessee Valley Authority was created and with public funds it built a series of dams for the creation of power which in turn was to be sold to municipalities and farm cooperatives for transmission. Unnecessary holding companies in electric light and power were to be eliminated.

10. Foreign trade was to be revived. An Export-Import Bank was devised to finance the flow of goods and to extend credit to foreign governments if need be. Reciprocal trading agreements, written by the State Department, were to be used to effect the lowering of tariff barriers everywhere, largely through the employment of the device of most-favored-nation treatment.

DEFICIT FINANCING

Lending and spending were the chief resorts of the New Deal in creating employment and revitalizing the economy. This resulted in deficit financing, for debt was augmented to obtain the required funds. It loaned to distressed banks, railroads, insurance companies, mortgage corporations, and industrial concerns. It loaned to farmers, home owners, municipalities. It loaned—or authorized them to raise funds directly—to the newly established public authorities. It spent, by appropriation, subsidy, and grant-in-aid, to rehabilitate marginal farmers, to finance the building of ships, to put up low-cost housing, to construct public buildings, to provide flood control, roads, and reforestation, to launch writers, painters, and theater-arts projects. All this gave people work, added to the social assets of the nation—and increased the public debt. Debt did not trouble the New Deal planners as long as the national income was increased. But what if debt and fiscal policy generally (through taxation) did not revive private investment; then how permanent could such accomplishments really be? This was the question that began to be raised notably after 1938.

POSITION OF AGRICULTURE

On many fronts, the problems of agriculture were explored and remedies sought. To increase farmer purchasing power, the concept of "parity prices" (later, "parity income") was devised in an effort to bringing farm purchasing power back to the levels of 1909–1914, when presumably agriculture was in balance with the rest of the economy. Farm production was to be adjusted to meet the needs of the market. Production was to be curtailed, and where surpluses appeared, they were to be held off the market by loans made to farmers. Also, soil conservation was to be pushed, mortgage debt was to be reduced, and efforts were to be made to rehabilitate marginal farmers.

The Agricultural Adjustment Act was passed in 1933 and continued on the statute books until 1936, when it was declared unconstitutional by the Supreme Court. Because overproduction was the difficulty, farmers were to receive "benefit payments" to encourage them to restrict plantings; funds for this purpose were to come from "processing taxes" on millers, cotton ginners, meat packers, and the like. It was this latter provision that the Supreme Court found illegal.

To continue controls and subsidies, the temporary Soil Conservation and Domestic Allotment Act and the Agricultural Adjustment Act of 1938 were passed. Both based government action on the necessity for protecting the land resources of the nation; subsidies—this time from government revenues—and loans were to continue. Both devices succeeded and agricultural prices —and the net income of farmers—began to rise. Net farm income stood at $6.1 billions in 1929, had fallen to $2 billions in 1932, and went up to $6 billions in 1937, dropping, however, to $4.5 billions in 1939. The parity ratio (percentage ratio of prices received by farmers to parity index) stood at 92 in 1929, had fallen to 58 in 1932, in 1937 stood at 93 and in 1939 at 77.

POSITION OF LABOR

The worker of the nation, to assure the establishment of collective-bargaining agencies and to create national minimums for wage and maximums for hours, received support from the National Labor Relations Act of 1935 and the Fair Labor Standards Act of 1938. The first required that employers bargain collectively with trade unions and surrender unfair labor practices; to enforce these requirements, a National Labor Relations Board was created which could decide which were the appropriate units for collective-bargaining purposes, conduct trade-union elections. and issue orders against the unfair conduct of management. The Fair Labor Standards Act established a 40-hour week (with time and a half for overtime), fixed 40 cents an hour as a minimum wage (raised to $1 an hour in 1956) and made possible the elimination of child labor by governmental order.

Trade unionism expanded under the AFL and the CIO (Committee, later Congress, for Industrial Organization). The latter, making its appearance in 1935, met with immediate successes in the unionization of the mass-production industries. The AFL also grew; in consequence, by 1941, each federation was claiming 4 million dues-paying members. The unions had direct impacts on salary increases and the adoption of fringe benefits (vacations with pay, retirement benefits, health insurance). It may very well be that during the 1930s, wages increased beyond productivity, reducing the marginal return of capital and therefore slowing down private investment. Thus, according to Professor Sumner H. Slichter, during 1921–1926, physical productivity per manhour in manufacturing increased 4.3 per cent a year, while hourly earnings increased 8.4 per cent. On the other hand, during 1933–1937, productivity per man hour went up only 1.7 per cent a year, while hourly earnings rose 40 per cent.

COURSE OF RECOVERY

As a result of all these efforts on the part of government—but largely due to deficit financing—recovery was of a mixed character, production moving up from 1933 to 1937 but slipping back badly in that year. With 1947–1949 as 100, the index of industrial production stood at 59 in 1929, 31 in 1932, 61 in 1937, and 48 in 1938. The figures for GNP [Gross National Product] (in billions of dollars, 1947 prices) were for the same years:

1929, $149.3 billions; 1932, $107.6 billions; 1937 $153.5 billions; 1938, $145.9 billions. On the other hand, the total labor force had increased from 49.4 millions in 1929 to 55 millions in 1938; in consequence, there continued to be sizable unemployment, possibly as much as 10 millions out of work. If recovery has been complete, and taking into consideration population increases and improvements in productivity during the decade (as much as 25 per cent), real GNP should have been fully 30 per cent higher.

Many factors contributed to the slowness of recovery. Higher labor costs, higher taxation, the mounting public debt bred no business confidence. There were charges being made that there was a "strike of capital," and this was probably so, because, despite all "easy money" efforts on the part of government, there was little significant increase in business loans.

The New Deal successes, as a result, were linked not so much with businss expansion as with government spending. When deficit financing slowed down, as it did in 1937, recession at once set in, and only the resumption of public spending in 1938 and 1939 brought back revival.

DEBT AND TAXES

Deficit financing was being pursued during the whole of the 1930s, and by the end of the decade the government debt had grown to more than $40 billions. This was largely due to an increase in expenditures. During 1931–1935, federal expenditures were in the neighborhood of $4 billions annually; in 1934, they were $6 billions; and in 1937, $8.4 billions. For the years 1931–1938, the total deficit was $20 billions.

Taxes mounted at the same time. Income taxes were pushed up, and in 1936, as a further tax on corporations, an undistributed-profits tax was levied. While this was abandoned in 1938, corporations nevertheless had little relief as far as losses were concerned. Federal taxes in 1931 came to $2.7 billions; in 1938, they were at $5.9 billions. The Revenue Acts, from 1932 to 1936, raised the maximum rate of the personal income tax from 25 to 79 per cent, the estate tax rate from a maximum of 20 to

70 per cent, imposed a new gifts tax with a maximum rate of 52 per cent, and increased the tax on capital gains. Arthur F. Burns, Chairman of the Council of Economic Advisers, commenting on this situation in 1956, pointed out: "These onerous taxes reduced the spending power of both individuals and businesses. Worse still, by coming in quick succession and creating uncertainty about the objectives of governmental policy, they weakened the incentives of businessmen and consumers to undertake capital expenditures. Innovation, private enterprise, and private investment languished."

All this was so. The other side of the shield was a willingness on the part of Americans to use the normal processes of discussion and action as they faced up to their difficulties. There was no widespread rejection of capitalist institutions as such. It was assumed, as a result of striving and experimentation, the American economy once more would begin its rise. This in fact, it did, from 1945 on. The Second World War intervened first.

6 FROM *Carl N. Degler*

The Establishment of the Guarantor State

Carl Degler, now a professor of history at Stanford University, represented the rise of a new generation in New Deal historiography—a generation that came of age during New Deal years. Born in Orange, New Jersey, in 1921, Degler was educated at Upsala College and Columbia University. After teaching in several eastern schools, he joined the history department at Vassar College, and while serving as an assistant professor there, he wrote the broad essay on American history from which the following selection is taken. Seeking to answer the question "How did Americans get to be the way they are in the middle of the

SOURCE. Abridged from pp. 379, 384–391, 400–413 of *Out of Our Past: The Forces that Shaped Modern America*, Revised Edition, by Carl N. Degler. Copyright 1959, 1970 by Carl N. Degler. By permission of Harper & Row, Publishers, Inc.

twentieth century?" Degler regarded the American story as a
success story and the New Deal as one of the successes.

The selection that follows is from the 1970 edition of the
book. His interpretation and presentation of the New Deal, how-
ever, had not changed since the essay's first appearance in 1959.
Like Hacker, he labeled it "The Third American Revolution."
His interpretation stressed several developments, including the
rise of Big Labor, but placed heaviest emphasis on the establish-
ment of Big Government, especially the "guarantor state."

Twice since the founding of the Republic, cataclysmic events
have sliced through the fabric of American life, snapping many
of the threads which ordinarily bind the past to the future. The
War for the Union was one such event, the Great Depression of
the 1930's the other. And, as the Civil War was precipitated
from the political and moral tensions of the preceding era, so the
Great Depression was a culmination of the social and economic
forces of industrialization and urbanization which had been
transforming America since 1865. A depression of such perva-
siveness as that of the thirties could happen only to a people already tightly interlaced by the multitudinous cords of a machine
civilization and embedded in the matrix of an urban society.

In all our history no other economic collapse brought so many
Americans to near starvation, endured so long, or came so close
to overturning the basic institutions of American life. It is understandable, therefore, that from that experience should issue a
new conception of the good society.

•   •   •

Perhaps the most striking alteration in American thought
which the depression fostered concerned the role of the government in the economy. Buffeted and bewildered by the economic
debacle, the American people in the course of the 1930's abandoned, once and for all, the doctrine of laissez faire. This beau
ideal of the nineteenth-century economists had become, ever
since the days of Jackson, an increasingly cherished shibboleth
of Americans. But now it was almost casually discarded. It is
true, of course, that the rejection of laissez faire had a long histo-

ry; certainly the Populists worked to undermine it. But with the depression the nation at large accepted the government as a permanent influence in the economy.

Almost every one of the best-known measures of the federal government during the depression era made inroads into the hitherto private preserves of business and the individual. Furthermore, most of these new measures survived the period, taking their places as fundamental elements in the structure of American life. For modern Americans living under a federal government of transcendent influence and control in the economy, this is the historic meaning of the great depression.

Much of what is taken for granted today as the legitimate function of government and the social responsibility of business began only with the legislation of these turbulent years. Out of the investigation of banking and bankers in 1933, for example, issued legislation which separated commercial banking from the stock and bond markets, and insured the bank deposits of ordinary citizens. The stock market, like the banks, was placed under new controls and a higher sense of responsibility to the public imposed upon it by the new Securities and Exchange Commission. The lesson of Black Tuesday in 1929 had not been forgotten; the classic free market itself—the Exchange—was hereafter to be under continuous governmental scrutiny.

The three Agricultural Adjustment Acts of 1933, 1936, and 1938, while somewhat diverse in detail, laid down the basic lines of what is still today the American approach to the agricultural problem. Ever since the collapse of the boom after the First World War, American agriculture had suffered from the low prices born of the tremendous surpluses. Unable to devise a method for expanding markets to absorb the excess, the government turned to restriction of output as the only feasible alternative. But because restriction of output meant curtailment of income for the farmer, it became necessary, if farm income was to be sustained, that farmers be compensated for their cut in production. Thus was inaugurated the singular phenomenon, which is still a part of the American answer to the agricultural surplus, of paying farmers for *not* growing crops. The other device introduced for raising farm prices, and still the mainstay of our farm policy, came with the 1938 act, which provided that the govern-

ment would purchase and store excess farm goods, thus supporting the price level by withdrawing the surplus from the competitive market. Both methods constitute a subsidy for the farmer
from society at large.

Though the Eisenhower administration in the 1950's called
for a return to a free market in farm products, at least in part—
that is, the removal of government supports from prices—Congress refused to go along. Under Kennedy and Johnson government
subsidy for agriculture has been continued as it undoubtedly
will be under the Nixon administration. A free market in agriculture was in operation during the twenties, but it succeeded
only in making farmers the economic stepchildren of an otherwise prosperous decade. Moreover, today the farm bloc is too
powerful politically to be treated so cavalierly. Furthermore, the
depression has taught most Americans—and western Europeans
as well—that a free market is not only a rarity in the modern
world, but that it is sometimes inimical to a stable and lasting
prosperity. All of the countries of western Europe also provide
government subsidies to agriculture.

Perhaps the most imaginative and fruitful innovation arising
out of the depression was the Tennessee Valley Authority, which
transformed the heart of the South. "It was and is literally a
down to earth experiment," native Tennesseean Broadus Mitchell has written, "with all that we know from test tube and loga-
rithm tables called on to help. It was a union of heart and mind
to restore what had been wasted. It was a social resurrection."
For the TVA was much more than flood and erosion control or
even hydroelectric power—though its gleaming white dams are
perhaps its most striking and best-known monuments. It was social planning of the most humane sort, where even the dead were
carefully removed from cemeteries before the waters backed up
behind the dams. It brought new ideas, new wealth, new skills,
new hope into a wasted, tired, and discouraged region.

At the time of the inception of the TVA, it was scarcely be-
lievable that the "backward" South would ever utilize all the
power the great dams would create. But in its report of 1956, the
Authority declared that the Valley's consumption of electricity
far exceeded that produced from water sites: almost three
quarters of TVA's power is now generated from steam power,

not from waterfall. In large part it was the TVA which taught the Valley how to use more power to expand its industries and to lighten the people's burdens. Back in 1935, Drew and Leon Pearson saw this creation of consumer demand in action. "Uncle Sam is a drummer with a commercial line to sell," they wrote in *Harper's Magazine*. "He sold liberty bonds before, but never refrigerators."

Measured against textbook definitions, the TVA is unquestionably socialism. The government owns the means of production and, moreover, it competes with private producers of electricity. But pragmatic Americans—and particularly those living in the Valley—have had few sleepless nights as a consequence of this fact. The TVA does its appointed job, and apparently it is here to stay. For when the Eisenhower administration sought to establish an alternative to the expansion of the TVA power facilities by awarding a contract for a steam plant to a private firm—Dixon-Yates—friends of the TVA in and out of Congress forced the cancellation of the contract. And despite Eisenhower's unfortunate reference to it as "creeping socialism," the TVA has been absorbed into that new American Way fashioned by the experimentalism of the American people out of the wreckage of the Great Depression.

Undoubtedly social security deserves the appellation "revolutionary" quite as much as the TVA; it brought government into the lives of people as nothing had since the draft and the income tax. Social security legislation actually comprises two systems: insurance against old age and insurance in the event of loss of work. The first system was completely organized and operated by the federal government; the second was shared with the states —but the national government set the standards; both were clear acknowledgment of the changes which had taken place in the family and in the business of making a living in America. No longer in urban America could the old folks, whose proportion in the society was steadily increasing, count on being taken in by their offspring as had been customary in a more agrarian world. Besides, such a makeshift arrangement was scarcely satisfying to the self-respect of the oldsters. With the transformation of the economy by industrialization, most Americans had become helpless before the vagaries of the business cycle. As a consequence of the social forces which were steadily augmenting social insecurity, only collective action by the government could arrest the drift.

To have the government concerned about the security of the individual was a new thing. Keenly aware of the novelty of this aim in individualistic America, Roosevelt was careful to deny any serious departure from traditional paths. "These three great objectives—the security of the home, the security of livelihood, and the security of social insurance," he said in 1934, constitute "a minimum of the promise that we can offer to the American people." But this, he quickly added, "does not indicate a change in values."

Whether the American people thought their values had changed is not nearly as important as the fact that they accepted social security. And the proof that they did is shown in the steady increase in the proportion of the population covered by the old-age benefit program since 1935; today farm workers as well as the great preponderance of nonfarm workers are included in the system. Apart from being a minimum protection for the individual and society against the dry rot of industrial idleness, unemployment insurance is now recognized as one of the major devices for warding off another depression.

It is true, as proponents of the agrarian life have been quick to point out, that an industrialized people, stripped as they are of their economic self-reliance, have felt the need for social insurance more than people in other types of society. But it is perhaps just as important to recognize that it is only in such a highly productive society that people can even dare to dream of social security. Men in other ages have felt the biting pains of economic crisis, but few preindustrial people have ever enjoyed that surfeit of goods which permits the fat years to fill out the lean ones. But like so much else concerning industrialism, it is not always easy to calculate whether the boons it offers exceed in value the burdens which it imposes.

For the average man, the scourge of unemployment was the essence of the depression. Widespread unemployment, permeating all ranks and stations in society, drove the American people and their government into some of their most determined and deliberate departures from the hallowed policy of "hands off."

But despite the determination, as late as 1938 the workless still numbered almost ten million—two thirds as great as in 1932 under President Hoover. The governmental policies of the 1930's never appreciably diminished the horde of unemployed—only the war prosperity of 1940 and after did that—but the providing of jobs by the federal government was a reflection of the people's new conviction that the government had a responsibility to alleviate economic disaster. Such bold action on the part of government, after the ineffective, if earnest approach of the Hoover administration, was a tonic for the dragging spirits of the people.

A whole range of agencies, from the Civil Works Administration (CWA) to the Works Progress Administration (WPA), were created to carry the attack against unemployment. It is true that the vast program of relief which was organized was not "permanent" in the sense that it is still in being, but for two reasons it deserves to be discussed here. First, since these agencies constituted America's principal weapon against unemployment, some form of them will surely be utilized if a depression should occur again. Second, the various relief agencies of the period afford the best examples of the new welfare outlook, which was then in the process of formation.

Though in the beginning relief programs were premised on little more than Harry Hopkins' celebrated dictum, "Hunger is not debatable," much more complex solutions to unemployment were soon worked out. The relief program of the WPA, which after 1935 was the major relief agency, was a case in point. In 1937, *Fortune* magazine commented on "the evolution of unemployment relief from tool to institution"—a recognition of the importance and duration of relief in America. "In 1936, the federal government was so deeply involved in the relief of the unemployed," *Fortune* contended, "that it was not only keeping them alive, but it was also giving them an opportunity to work; and not only giving them an opportunity to work but giving them an opportunity to work at jobs for which they were peculiarly fitted; and not only giving them an opportunity to work at jobs for which they were peculiarly fitted, but creating for them jobs of an interest and usefulness which they could not have expected to find in private employment." The statement somewhat distorts the work of the WPA, but it sums up the main outlines of the evolution of the relief program.

The various artistic and cultural employment programs of the WPA are excellent examples of how relief provided more than employment, though any of the youth agencies like the Civilian Conservation Corps or the National Youth Administration (it subsidized student work) would serve equally well. At its peak, the Federal Writers' Project employed some 6,000 journalists, poets, novelists, and Ph.D.'s of one sort or another; unknowns worked on the same payroll, if not side by side, with John Steinbeck, Vardis Fisher, and Conrad Aiken. The $46 million expended on art—that is, painting and sculpture—by the WPA in 1936–37 exceeded the artistic budget of any country outside the totalitarian orbit—and there art was frankly propagandistic. *Fortune*, in May, 1937, found the American government's sponsorship of art singularly free of censorship or propaganda. The magazine concluded that "by and large the Arts Projects have been given a freedom no one would have thought possible in a government run undertaking. And by and large that freedom has not been abused." During the first fifteen months of the Federal Music Project, some fifty million people heard live concerts; in the first year of the WPA Theater, sixty million people in thirty states saw performances, with weekly attendance running to half a million. T. S. Eliot's *Murder in the Cathedral*, too risky for a commercial producer, was presented in New York by the Federal Theater to 40,000 people at a top price of 55 cents.

"What the government's experiments in music, painting, and the theater actually did," concluded *Fortune* in May, 1937, "even in their first year, was to work a sort of cultural revolution in America." For the first time the American audience and the American artist were brought face to face for their mutual benefit. "Art in America is being given its chance," said the British writer Ford Madox Ford, "and there has been nothing like it since before the Reformation. . . ."

Instead of being ignored on the superficially plausible grounds of the exigencies of the depression, the precious skills of thousands of painters, writers, and musicians were utilized. By this timely rescue of skills, tastes, and talents from the deadening hand of unemployment, the American people, through their government, showed their humanity and social imagination. Important for the future was the foresight displayed in the conserving of artistic talents and creations for the enrichment of generations to come.

The entrance of the federal government into a vast program of relief work was an abrupt departure from all previous practice, but it proved enduring. "When President Roosevelt laid it down that government had a social responsibility to care for the victims of the business cycle," *Fortune* remarked prophetically in 1937, "he set in motion an irreversible process." The burden of unemployment relief was too heavy to be carried by local government or private charities in an industrialized society; from now on, the national government would be expected to shoulder the responsibility. "Those who are on relief and in close contact otherwise with public matters realize that what has happened to the country is a bloodless revolution," wrote an anonymous relief recipient in *Harper's* in 1936. The government, he said, has assumed a new role in depressions, and only the rich might still be oblivious to it. But they too "will know it by 1940. And in time," they will "come to approve the idea of everyone having enough to eat." Few people escaped the wide net of the depression: "anybody sinks after a while," the anonymous reliefer pointed out. "Even you would have if God hadn't preserved, without apparent rhyme or reason, your job and your income." That the depression was threat to all was perhaps the first lesson gained from the 1930's.

The second was that only through collective defense could such a threat be met. By virtue of the vigorous attack made upon the economic problems of the thirties by the government, the age-old conviction that dips in the business cycle were either the will of God or the consequence of unalterable economic laws was effectively demolished. As recently as 1931, President Hoover had told an audience that some people "have indomitable confidence that by some legerdemain we can legislate ourselves out of a world-wide depression. Such views are as accurate as the belief that we can exorcise a Caribbean hurricane." From the experience of the depression era, the American people learned that something could and ought to be done when economic disaster strikes. No party and no politician with a future will ever again dare to take the fatalistic course of Herbert Hoover in 1929–1933.

•   •   •

. . . Instead of killing off many unions, as depressions had done earlier, the depression of the thirties seemed to stimulate a new and aggressive organizing spirit among the workers. In the light of the later tremendous expansion of union membership, it might be said that the depression created a class consciousness among American workingmen for the first time sufficient to permit large-scale unionization.

Despite the fact that the vast majority of unionized workers were then in the American Federation of Labor, that body was not destined to be the instrument of the new unionization. The Federation was too cautious, too saturated with Samuel Gompers' commitment to craft forms of organization and his fear of governmental interference, to be able to capitalize on the unrest among the workers. It is true that some Federation leaders like John L. Lewis of the Miners and Hillman of the Clothing Workers were pressing hard for new organizing drives among the workers of the still unorganized great industries of the country like textiles, steel, rubber, automobiles, and aircraft. But such men were a small minority in the Federation.

The deepening of the economic slump, however, did open crevices in the Federation's high wall of tradition. At the 1932 convention in Cincinnati, John L. Lewis convinced the convention to go on record in favor of state unemployment systems. To the old-timers in the Federation this was a serious and dangerous departure from Gompers' inflexible principle of "voluntarism" —that is, no government interference on either side in the match between capital and labor. Lewis also cajoled the delegates—apparently bewildered and shaken by the enormity of the economic crisis—into accepting the principle of a legislatively limited working day—a further repudiation of Gompers' principles.

Then came the opening notes of the Rooseveltian performance, foremost among which was the National Industrial Recovery Act. This measure contained a labor clause—the well-known 7a—which guaranteed to workers the right of free choice of union and committed the employers to dealing with such unions.

Spurred by this government encouragement, both spontaneous organization and A.F. of L.-affiliated unionization surged forward. More than 1,100 federal and local unions in the mass production industries of automobiles, aluminum, and rubber were brought into being by 1935; union membership for these industries shot up from less than 1,000 in 1933 to over ten times that figure in 1935. President Green of the A.F. of L. announced that between 60,000 and 70,000 workers had been added to the Federation in Akron alone in 1933, most of them in the rubber industry. Capitalizing on Roosevelt's acceptance of section 7a, John L. Lewis told the miners, "The President wants you to join a union." The United Mine Workers, though wasting away all through the twenties, attracted 300,000 members to its rolls in the spring and early summer of 1933. The Ladies Garment Workers Union added 100,000; the Amalgamated Clothing Workers gathered in another 50,000 during the middle months of NRA's first year. At the A.F. of L. convention of 1934, the Executive Council reported "a virtual uprising of workers for union membership. Workers," the Council said with amazement, "held mass meetings and sent word they wanted to be organized."

The emphasis on craft organization and the cautious philosophy of the American Federation of Labor, however, were not equal to the task of organizing and canalizing this upsurge among the workers in the mass production industries. The craft form, where unionization proceeded along the lines of the job, rather than the factory, made no sense whatsoever in any of the great industries where the mass of workers were semiskilled or unskilled rather than skilled. Moreover, to divide the workers in a plant according to occupations resulted in endless jurisdictional disputes among the unions. Ultimately the mishandling of the organizational problem reflected itself in loss of membership. For example, though in 1934 the A.F. of L. had over 150,000 members in its 100 locals in the automobile industry, by 1936 the membership had dwindled away to 19,000. A willingness to try new forms and to include the unskilled and semiskilled, who bulked so large in the mass production industries, was urgently needed if organized labor was to benefit from the workers' new interest in unions.

The obvious failure of the A.F. of L.'s approach to the mass industries came to a head in the heated Atlantic City convention of October, 1935. Beetle-browed, leonine John L. Lewis of the industrially organized Miners raised his stentorian voice in behalf of the unorganized. "Heed this cry from Macedonia that comes from the hearts of men," he cried to the impassive leaders of labor's elite. "Organize the unorganized and in doing this make the A.F. of L. the greatest instrument that has ever been forged to befriend the cause of humanity and champion human rights." Defeated at every turn on the floor of the convention (except perhaps in his famous right hook to the nose of arch-conservative William Hutcheson of the Carpenters), Lewis and his fellow rebels, the day after the convention closed, organized the Committee for Industrial Organization. Composed of ten of the more aggressive and spirited of the A.F. of L. unions, this committee sparked the mighty organizing effort which transformed American industrial and labor relations in the next handful of years. Within a year after the formation of the C.I.O., the A.F. of L. expelled the constituent unions. The split in the labor movement, destined to remain unhealed for twenty years, was a fact.

In view of the consequences, however, that split was the most promising thing that ever happened to Samuel Gompers' beloved American Federation of Labor in particular and to the American workingman in general. The C.I.O.—formed into the permanent Congress of Industrial Organizations in 1938—undertook a massive and energetic invasion of unorganized mass industries like steel, automobiles, textiles, rubber, aircraft, and lumber—all industries which had implacably resisted the union organizer for over a generation. One by one, with varying degrees of violence and resistance, they fell to the determination, the guts, and the persistence of the new unionism. In time the A.F. of L. also joined in, and by 1940 total union membership in the country had risen to 8.5 million from 3.7 million only five years earlier. Under the impact of the depression, the American labor movement had come of age.

Aside from the new and vital spirit which the C.I.O. breathed into the labor movement, its great innovation was its effective use of the industrial-union form. So successfully was this form adapted to the economic structure that the industrial union soon captured a prominent place in the once craft-dominated A.F. of L. By 1940 about a quarter of the A.F. of L.'s four million members were in industrial unions and a quarter of the C.I.O.'s workers were in craft unions. Furthermore, by organizing recent immigrants, the unskilled, Negroes, and women on a scale and with a determination never attempted by the A.F. of L., the C.I.O. revived a broad approach to unionism which had been sidetracked in America ever since the A.F. of L. had beaten out the old Knights of Labor.

The enormous expansion of unionization in the last years of the depression was not solely attributable to the novel spirit among the unions and the workers. Much of the impetus came from the new attitude of the government. We have already seen the catalytic effect the NRA had on the rush toward unionization, and it would be difficult to exaggerate that effect. When that act was declared unconstitutional in 1935, its place was taken by the National Labor Relations Act (the Wagner Act), in itself perhaps the most revolutionary single measure in American labor history.

The Wagner Act started from the same premise as section 7a of the NRA—that is, that workers should be free to choose their own unions and employers must abstain from interfering in this choice. It also required that employers accept duly constituted unions as legitimate representatives of their employees and bargain with them. The act also set up a board—the National Labor Relations Board—whose duty it was to supervise elections for the certification of unions as representatives of a majority of the workers in a plant, and to hear complaints against employers for having interfered with union organizing. The Board was also empowered to hear complaints against employers for refusing to bargain with a certified union.

In two different ways, the act threw the enormous prestige and power of the government behind the drive for organizing workers. In the first place, it flatly declared unionization to be a desirable thing for the national economy, forbidding employers to interfere in the process of organization. Five so-called unfair labor practices were listed, all of them acts which only an employer could commit; the act listed no "unfair" practices of labor. (Actually, the courts had built up such a large body of common-law interpretations of unfair labor practices by unions that it was hardly necessary to add to them in the act.) Moreover, as an additional indication of its belief in the labor movement, the law virtually outlawed the company union—that is, the labor organization sponsored by the employer. In the second place, once a union was formed, and it had been certified by the Board as speaking for a majority of the workers, the employer, under the act, had no alternative but to recognize it as the representative of his employees. Though it is true that many employers refused to accept the constitutionality of the law—usually on the advice of their lawyers—until after the Supreme Court decision of 1937 in the Jones and Laughlin Steel case, this placing of the government on the side of unionization was of central importance in the success of many an organizational drive of the C.I.O., notably those against Ford and Little Steel.

The passage of this controversial act marked, insofar as labor was concerned, an acceptance of governmental assistance which would have made old Sam Gompers apoplectic. All during his leadership of the A.F. of L., labor had consistently refused to accept (except for the war emergency) government intervention at the bargaining table of labor and business. But by accepting governmental assistance, the American labor movement not only departed from its own traditions, but from those of European labor as well. Although well aware of the benefits to be derived from such government support as the American movement received, labor in England and on the Continent has not abandoned its historic independence of the state. European labor unions have preferred to remain untouched by the quasi-governmental status in which the American labor movement has permitted itself to be clothed. Labor's bête noire, the Taft-Hartley Act, is an obvious confirmation of the truism that dependence on government is a knife which cuts both ways.

●　　●　　●

So lusty and powerful did organized labor grow under the new dispensation that by the time the Second World War was over, a strong movement was afoot to amend the Wagner Act in order to protect the interests of the employer and to secure the national welfare against certain powerful national unions. The result was the Taft-Hartley Act of 1947, actually an amendment to the original 1935 act. Without entering into the details, suffice it to say that this amendment now added certain unfair labor practices of which unions might be guilty, such as the secondary boycott, and bestowed special powers upon the federal government for effectively handling paralyzing nationwide strikes. But the central core of the National Labor Relations Act was left unimpaired, as it remains today. The American people under Republican as well as Democratic regimes have reaffirmed more than once the principle that it is the obligation of the federal government to protect a worker in the free exercise of the right to join a union and that all employers must bargain collectively with a certified union.

Enormous as was the assistance which labor received from government in the form of the NLRA, there was still another piece of legislation which offered a boost to labor. This was the Wages and Hours Act of 1938, which set minimum wages and maximum hours for workers in industries engaged in interstate commerce. Since its example has been followed by several industrial states like New York, the principle of a legislative floor under wages and a ceiling on hours has been extended beyond the constitutional limits of the federal government's power. Because the minimum set by law was well below the going industrial wage, the act did not affect most workers, but it helped considerably to pull up wages in certain unorganized industries. Furthermore, it helped to narrow the wage differences between northern and southern industries. During the first two years of the act, nearly a million workers received increased wages under its provisions and over three million had their hours shortened. Subsequent to that time, the minimum wage has been progressively increased from the original 40 cents an hour to the present (1968) $1.60, thereby putting a rising floor under the nation's industrial wage scale. Furthermore, in abolishing child labor in all industries involved in interstate commerce, the act achieved a long-sought goal of the labor and liberal movements in the United States. And once again, it is worth noticing, it was accomplished through the powerful intervention of an active federal government.

Seen against a broader canvas, the depression, together with government support, profoundly altered the position of labor in

American society. Girded with its new-found power and protections, Big Labor now took its place beside Big Business and Big Government to complete a triumvirate of economic power. And when it is recognized that through the so-called farm bloc in Congress agriculture also has attained a sort of veto power on the operations of the economic system, it is not difficult to appreciate the aptness of John Galbraith's description of modern American capitalism as a system of "countervailing power." Instead of competition being the regulator of the economic system, Professor Galbraith persuasively argues, we now have a system of economic checks and balances—Big Labor, Big Business, Big Agriculture, and so forth—no one of which is big enough or powerful enough to control the total economy. Though Galbraith's argument is not totally convincing, his conception of the American economy is much closer to reality than is the old competitive model. And insofar as Professor Galbraith's analysis is correct, it is clear that this system of countervailing power came into being during the depression, with the rise of Big Government, Organized Agriculture, and Big Labor.

•　　•　　•

In the thirties, as now, the place of the New Deal in the broad stream of American development has been a matter of controversy. Historians and commentators on the American scene have not yet reached a firm agreement—if they ever will—as to whether the New Deal was conservative or radical in character. Certainly if one searches the writings and utterances of Franklin Roosevelt, his own consciousness of conservative aims is quickly apparent. "The New Deal is an old deal—as old as the earliest aspirations of humanity for liberty and justice and the good life," he declared in 1934. "It was this administration," he told a Chicago audience in 1936, "which saved the system of private profit and free enterprise after it had been dragged to the brink of ruin. . . ."

But men making a revolution among a profoundly conservative people do not advertise their activity, and above all Franklin Roosevelt understood the temper of his people. Nor should such a statement be interpreted as an insinuation of high conspiracy —far from it. Roosevelt was at heart a conservative, as his lifelong interest in history, among other things, suggests. But he was without dogma in his conservatism, which was heavily interlaced with genuine concern for people. He did not shy away from new means and new approaches to problems when circumstances demanded it. His willingness to experiment, to listen to his university-bred Brains trust, to accept a measure like the TVA, reveal the flexibility in his thought. Both his lack of theoretical presuppositions and his flexibility are to be seen in the way he came to support novel measures like social security and the Wagner Act. Response to popular demand was the major reason. "The Congress can't stand the pressure of the Townsend Plan unless we have a real old-age insurance system." he complained to Frances Perkins, "nor can I face the country without having . . . a solid plan which will give some assurance to old people of systematic assistance upon retirement." In like manner, the revolutionary NLRA was adopted as a part of his otherwise sketchy and rule-of-thumb philosophy of society. Though ultimately Roosevelt championed the Wagner bill in the House, it was a belated conversion dictated by the foreshadowed success of the measure and the recent invalidation of the NRA. In his pragmatic and common-sense reactions to the exigencies of the depression, Roosevelt, the easy-going conservative, ironically enough became the embodiment of a new era and a new social philosophy for the American people.

"This election," Herbert Hoover presciently said in 1932, "is not a mere shift from the ins to the outs. It means deciding the direction our nation will take over a century to come." The election of Franklin Roosevelt, he predicted, would result in "a radical departure from the foundations of 150 years which have made this the greatest nation in the world." Though Hoover may be charged with nothing more than campaign flourishing, it is nevertheless a fact that his speech was made just after Roosevelt's revealing Commonwealth Club address of September. Only in this single utterance, it should be remembered, did Roosevelt disclose in clear outline the philosophy and program which was later to be the New Deal. "Every man has a right to life," he had said, "and this means that he has also a right to make a comfortable living. . . . Our government, formal and informal, political and economic," he went on, "owes to everyone an avenue to possess himself of a portion of that plenty [from our industrial society] sufficient for his needs, through his own work." Here were the intimations of those new goals which the New Deal set for America.

Accent as heavily as one wishes the continuity between the reforms of the Progressive era and the New Deal, yet the wide difference between the goals of the two periods still remains. The Progressive impulse was narrowly reformist: it limited business, it assisted agriculture, it freed labor from some of the shackles imposed by the courts, but it continued to conceive of the state as policeman or judge and nothing more. The New Deal, on the other hand, was more than a regulator—though it was that too, as shown by the SEC and the reinvigoration of the antitrust division of the Justice Department. To the old goals for America set forth and fought for by the Jeffersonians and the Progressives the New Deal appended new ones. Its primary and general innovation was the guaranteeing of a minimum standard of welfare for the people of the nation. WPA and the whole series of relief agencies which were a part of it, wages and hours legislation, AAA, bank deposit insurance, and social security, each illustrates this new conception of the federal government. A resolution offered by New Deal Senator Walsh in 1935 clearly enunciated the new obligations of government. The resolution took notice of the disastrous effects of the depression "upon the lives of young men and women . . ." and then went on to say that "it is the duty of the Federal Government to use every possible means of opening up opportunities" for the youth of the nation "so that they may be rehabilitated and restored to *a decent standard of living* and ensured proper development of their talents. . . ."

But the guarantor state as it developed under the New Deal was more active and positive than this. It was a vigorous and dynamic force in the society, energizing and, if necessary, supplanting private enterprise when the general welfare required it. With the Wagner Act, for example, the government served notice that it would actively participate in securing the unionization of the American worker; the state was no longer to be an impartial policeman merely keeping order; it now declared for the side of labor. When social and economic problems like the rehabilitation of the Valley of the Tennessee were ignored or shirked by private enterprise, then the federal government undertook to do the job. Did private enterprise fail to provide adequate and sufficient housing for a minimum standard of welfare for the people, then the government would build houses. As a result, boasted Nathan Straus, head of the U.S. Housing Authority, "for the first time in a hundred years the slums of America ceased growing and began to shrink."

Few areas of American life were beyond the touch of the experimenting fingers of the New Deal; even the once sacrosanct domain of prices and the valuation of money felt the tinkering. The devaluation of the dollar, the gold-purchase program, the departure from the gold standard—in short, the whole monetary policy undertaken by F. D. R. as a means to stimulate recovery through a price rise—constituted an unprecedented repudiation of orthodox public finance. To achieve that minimum standard of well-being which the depression had taught the American people to expect of their government, nothing was out of bounds.

But it is not the variety of change which stamps the New Deal as the creator of a new America; its significance lies in the permanence of its program. For, novel as the New Deal program was, it has, significantly, not been repudiated by the Eisenhower administration, the first Republican government since the reforms were instituted. Verbally, it is true, the Republican administration has had to minimize its actual commitments to the New Deal philosophy, and it tended to trust private business more than the New Dealers did—witness, for example, its elimination of the minor governmental manufacturing enterprises which competed with private firms. But despite this, the administration's firm commitment to the guaranteeing of prosperity and averting depression at all costs is an accurate reflection of the American people's agreement with the New Deal's diagnosis of the depression. Nor has the Republican party dared to repeal or even emasculate the legislation which made up the vitals of the New Deal: TVA, banking and currency, SEC, social security, the Wagner Act, and fair treatment of the Negro. The New Deal Revolution has become so much a part of the American Way that no political party which aspires to high office dares now to repudiate it.

• • •

The conclusion seems inescapable that, traditional as the words may have been in which the New Deal expressed itself, in actuality it was truly a revolution in ideas, institutions and practices, when one compares it with the political and social world that preceded it. In its long history, America has passed through two revolutions since the first one in 1776, but only the last two, the Civil War and the depression, were of such force as to change the direction of the relatively smooth flow of its progress. The Civil War rendered a final and irrevocable decision in the long debate over the nature of the Union and the position of the Negro in American society. From that revolutionary experience, America emerged a strong national state and dedicated by the words of its most hallowed document to the inclusion of the black man in a democratic culture. The searing ordeal of the Great Depression purged the American people of their belief in the limited powers of the federal government and convinced them of the necessity of the guarantor state. And as the Civil War constituted a watershed in American thought, so the depression and its New Deal marked the crossing of a divide from which, it would seem, there could be no turning back.

7 FROM   *Arthur M. Schlesinger, Jr.*
                   A Successful Middle Way

Schlesinger also represented a new generation in New Deal historiography but he did not represent a "generation gap." His interpretation of the New Deal was very close to his father's, though much more fully developed and documented. Born in Columbus, Ohio, in 1917, he was closely associated with his father until the latter's death. He was educated at Harvard while his father was a member of the faculty there; he joined his father as a member of Harvard's history department, and shared his father's liberalism and involvement in Democratic politics.

SOURCE. Arthur M. Schlesinger, Jr., *The Age of Roosevelt: The Politics of Upheaval*, Boston: Houghton Mifflin Co., 1960, pp. 647–654. Copyright © 1960 by Arthur M. Schlesinger, Jr. Reprinted by permission of the publisher, Houghton Mifflin Company.

The younger Schlesinger was more actively involved in politics. He was a leader in the Americans for Democratic Action, a liberal organization to which his father also belonged, and the author of one of the most important expressions of postwar liberalism, The Vital Center, *published in 1949, and he served on Adali Stevenson's campaign staff. Work on his massive study* The Age of Roosevelt, *which in three volumes carried the domestic history of the 1930's through the election of 1936, was interrupted by service as a special assistant to Presidents Kennedy and Johnson, the writing of a large work on Kennedy's presidency, which won him his second Pulitzer Prize, and participation in the political controversies of the late 1960's and early 1970's. His identification with his definition of the philosophy of Roosevelt and the New Deal is very obvious in the following selection.*

The assumption that there were two absolutely distinct economic orders, capitalism and socialism, expressed, of course, an unconscious Platonism—a conviction that reality inhered in theoretical essences of which any working economy, with its compromises and confusions, could only be an imperfect copy. If in the realm of essences capitalism and socialism were wholly separate phenomena based on wholly separate principles, then they must be rigorously kept apart on earth. Thus abstractions became more "real" than empirical reality: both doctrinaire capitalists and doctrinaire socialists fell victim to what Whitehead called the "fallacy of misplaced concreteness." Both ideological conservatism and ideological radicalism dwelt in the realm of either-or. Both preferred essence to existence.

The distinction of the New Deal lay precisely in its refusal to approach social problems in terms of ideology. Its strength lay in its preference of existence to essence. The great central source of its energy was the instinctive contempt of practical, energetic, and compassionate people for dogmatic absolutes. Refusing to be intimidated by abstractions or to be overawed by ideology, the New Dealers responded by doing things. Walt Whitman once wrote, "To work for Democracy is good, the exercise is good—strength it makes and lessons it teaches." The whole point of the

New Deal lay in its faith in "the exercise of Democracy," its belief in gradualness, its rejection of catastrophism, its denial of either-or, its indifference to ideology, its conviction that a managed and modified capitalist order achieved by piecemeal experiment could best combine personal freedom and economic growth. "In a world in which revolutions just now are coming easily," said Adolf Berle, "the New Deal chose the more difficult course of moderation and rebuilding." "It looks forward toward a more stable social order," said Morgenthau, "but it is not doctrinaire, not a complete cut-and-dried program. It involves the courage to experiment." "The course that the new administration did take," wrote Ickes, "was the hardest course. It conformed to no theory, but it did fit into the American system—to meet concrete needs, a system of courageous recognition of change." Tugwell, rejecting laissez faire and Communism, spoke of the "third course." *Hold Fast the Middle Way* was the title of a book by John Dickinson.

Roosevelt hoped to steer between the extreme of chaos and tyranny by moving always, in his phrase, "slightly to the left of center." "Unrestrained individualism" had proved a failure; yet "any paternalistic system which tries to provide for security for everyone from above only calls for an impossible task and a regimentation utterly uncongenial to the spirit of our people." He deeply agreed with Macaulay's injunction to reform if you would preserve. Once defending public housing to a press conference, he said, "If you had knowledge of what happened in Germany and England and Vienna, you would know that 'socialism' has probably done more to prevent Communism and rioting and revolution than anything else in the last four or five years."

Roosevelt had no illusions about revolution. Mussolini and Stalin seemed to him "not mere distant relatives" but "blood brothers." When Emil Ludwig asked him his "political motive," he replied, "My desire to obviate revolution. . . . I work in a contrary sense to Rome and Moscow." He said during the 1932 campaign:

"Say that civilization is a tree which, as it grows, continually produces rot and dead wood. The radical says: 'Cut it down.' The conservative says: 'Don't touch it.' The liberal compromises: 'Let's prune, so that we lose neither the old trunk nor the new branches.' This campaign is waged to teach the country to march upon its appointed course, the way of change, in an orderly march, avoiding alike the revolution of radicalism and the revolution of conservatism."

His "speech material" file contained a miscellany of material indexed according to the random categories of the President's mind. One folder bore the revealing label: "Liberalism vs. Communism and Conservatism."

As Roosevelt saw it, he was safeguarding the constitutional system by carrying through reforms long overdue. "The principal object of every Government all over the world," he once said, "seems to have been to impose the ideas of the last generation upon the present one. That's all wrong." As early as 1930 he had considered it time for America "to become fairly radical for at least one generation. History shows that where this occurs occasionally, nations are saved from revolution." In 1938 he remarked, "In five years I think we have caught up twenty years. If liberal government continues over another ten years we ought to be contemporary somewhere in the late nineteen forties."

For Roosevelt, the technique of liberal government was pragmatism. Tugwell talked about creating "a philosophy to fit the Rooseveltian method"; but this was the aspiration of an intellectual. Nothing attracted Roosevelt less than rigid intellectual systems. "The fluidity of change in society has always been the despair of theorists," Tugwell once wrote. This fluidity was Roosevelt's delight, and he floated upon it with the confidence of an expert sailor, who could detect currents and breezes invisible to others, hear the slap of waves on distant rocks, smell squalls beyond the horizon and make infallible landfalls in the blackest of fogs. He respected clear ideas, accepted them, employed them, but was never really at ease with them and always ultimately skeptical about their relationship to reality.

His attitude toward economists was typical. Though he acknowledged their necessity, he stood in little awe of them. "I brought down several books by English economists and leading American economists," he once told a press conference. ". . . I suppose I must have read different articles by fifteen different experts. Two things stand out: The first is that no two of them agree, and the other thing is that they are so foggy in what they say that it is almost impossible to figure out what they mean. It is jargon; absolute jargon." Once Roosevelt remarked to Keynes of Leon Henderson, "Just look at Leon. When I got him, he was only an economist." (Keynes could hardly wait to repeat this to Henderson.) Roosevelt dealt proficiently with practical questions of government finance, as he showed in his press conferences on the budget; but abstract theory left him cold.

Considering the state of economic theory in the nineteen thirties, this was not necessarily a disabling prejudice. Roosevelt had, as J. K. Galbraith has suggested, what was more important than theory, and surely far more useful than bad theory, a set of intelligent economic attitudes. He believed in government as an instrument for effecting economic change (though not as an instrument for doing everything: in 1934, he complained to the National Emergency Council, "There is the general feeling that it is up to the Government to take care of everybody . . . they should be told all the different things the Government can not do"). He did not regard successful businessmen as infallible repositories of economic wisdom. He regarded the nation as an estate to be improved for those who would eventually inherit it. He was willing to try nearly anything. And he had a sense of the complex continuities of history—that special intimacy with the American past which, as Frances Perkins perceptively observed, signified a man who had talked with old people who had talked with older people who remembered many things back to the War of the Revolution.

From this perspective, Roosevelt could not get excited about the debate between the First and Second New Deals. No one knew what he really thought about the question of the organic economy versus the restoration of competition. Tugwell, perhaps the most vigilant student of Roosevelt's economic ideas, could in one mood pronounce Roosevelt "a progressive of the nineteenth century in economic matters" (1946) who "clung to the Brandeis-Frankfurter view" (1950) and "could be persuaded away from the old progressive line only in the direst circumstances" (1950); in another, he could speak of Roosevelt's "preference for a planned and disciplined business system" (1957) and for "overhead management of the whole economy" (1940), and question whether he ever believed in Brandeis (1957). Corcoran and Cohen, who helped persuade Roosevelt to the Second New Deal, thought he never really abandoned the NRA dream of directing the economy through some kind of central economic mechanism. Roosevelt himself, confronted with a direct question, always wriggled away ("Brandeis is one thousand per cent right in principle but in certain fields there must be a guiding or restraining hand of Government because of the very nature of the specific field"). He never could see why the United States has to be all one way or all the other. "This country is big enough to experiment with several diverse systems and follow several different lines," he once remarked to Adolf Berle. "Why must we put our economic policy in a single systemic strait jacket?"

Rejecting the battle between the New Nationalism and the New Freedom which had so long divided American liberalism, Roosevelt equably defined the New Deal as the "saisfactory combination" of both. Rejecting the platonic distinction between "capitalism" and "socialism," he led the way toward a new society which took elements from each and rendered both obsolescent. It was this freedom from dogma which outraged the angry, logical men who saw everything with dazzling certitude. Roosevelt's illusion, said Herbert Hoover, was "that any economic system would work in a mixture of others. No greater illusions ever mesmerized the American people." "Your President," said Leon Trotsky with contempt, "abhors 'systems' and 'generalities.' . . . Your philosophic method is even more antiquated than your economic system." But the American President always resisted ideological commitment. His determination was to keep options open within the general frame of a humanized democracy; and his belief was that the very diversity of systems strengthened the basis for freedom.

Without some critical vision, pragmatism could be a meaningless technique; the flight from ideology, a form of laziness; the middle way, an empty conception. For some politicians, such an approach meant nothing more than splitting the difference between extremes; the middle of the road was thus determined by the clamor from each side. At times it appeared to mean little more than this to Roosevelt. But at bottom he had a guiding vision with substantive content of its own. The content was not, however, intellectual; and this was where he disappointed more precise and exacting minds around him. It was rather a human content, a sense of the fortune and happiness of people. In 1936 a Canadian editor asked him to state his objectives. Roosevelt's off-the-cuff reply defined his goal in all its naïveté and power:

". . . to do what any honest Government of any country would do; try to increase the security and the happiness of a larger number of people in all occupations of life and in all parts of the country; to give them more of the good things of life, to give them a greater distribution not only of wealth in the narrow terms, but of wealth in the wider terms; to give them places to go in the summer time—recreation; to give them assurance that they are not going to starve in their old age; to give honest business a chance to go ahead and make a reasonable profit, and to give everyone a chance to earn a living."

The listing was neither considered nor comprehensive, but the spirit was accurate. "The intellectual and spiritual climate," said Frances Perkins, "was Roosevelt's general attitude that *the people mattered.*" Nothing else would count until ordinary people were provided an environment and an opportunity "as good as human ingenuity can devise and fit for children of God."

Developed against the backdrop of depression, his philosophy of compassion had a particular bias toward the idea of security —"a greater physical and mental and spiritual security for the people of this country." "Security," he once said,

"means a kind of feeling within our individual selves that we have lacked all through the course of history. We have had to take our chance about our old age in days past. We have had to take our chance with depressions and boom times. We have had to take chances on buying our homes. I have believed for a great many years that the time has come in our civilization when a great many of these chances should be eliminated from our lives."

The urgencies of depression carried the concern for security to a degree which later generations, who thought they could assume abundance and move on to problems of opportunity and self-fulfillment, would find hard to understand. The old American dream, Roosevelt told a collection of young people in 1935, was the dream of the golden ladder—each individual for himself. But the newer generation would have a different dream: "Your advancement, you hope, is along a broad highway on which thousands of your fellow men and women are advancing with you." In many ways this was a dispiriting hope. In the longer run, security, while indispensable as a social minimum, might be cloying and perhaps even stultifying as a social ideal.

But this was a nuance imposed by depression. His essential ideals had an old-fashioned flavor. He was unconsciously seeing America in the Jeffersonian image of Dutchess County and Hyde Park. He hoped, as he said, to extend "to our national life the old principal of the local community, the principle that no individual, man, woman or child, has a right to do things that hurt his neighbors." "Our task of reconstruction does not require the creation of new and strange values. It is rather the finding of the way once more to known, but to some degree forgotten ideals." He wanted to make other people happy as he had been happy himself. Lifting his right hand high, his left hand only a little, he would say, "This difference is too big, it must become smaller—like this. . . . Wasn't I able to study, travel, take care of my sickness? The man who doesn't have to worry about his daily bread is securer and freer." He spoke of his philosophy as "social-mindedness." He meant by this essentially the humanization of industrial society.

A viewpoint so general provided no infallible guide to daily decision. Roosevelt therefore had to live by trial and error. His first term had its share of error: the overextension of NRA; the fumbling with monetary policy; the reluctant approach to spending; the waste of energy in trying to achieve the communitarian dream; the bungling of the London Economic Conference; the administrative confusion and conflict; the excessive reliance on ballyhoo and oratory. At times Roosevelt seemed almost to extemporize for the joy of it; his pragmatism appeared an addition to playing by ear in the nervous conviction that any kind of noise was better than silence. "Instead of being alarmed by the spirit of improvisation," wrote George Creel, "he seemed delighted by it, whooping on the improvisers with the excitement of one riding to hounds."

The chronic changing of front exposed the New Deal to repeated charges that it had no core of doctrine, that it was improvised and opportunistic, that it was guided only by circumstance. These charges were all true. But they also represented the New Deal's strength. For the advantage enjoyed by the pragmatists over the ideologists was their exceptional sensitivity to social and human reality. They measured results in terms not of conformity to *a priori* models but of concrete impact on people's lives. The New Deal thus had built-in mechanisms of feed-back, readjustment, and self-correction. Its incoherences were considerably more faithful to a highly complicated and shifting reality than any preconceived dogmatic system could have been. In the welter of confusion and ignorance, experiment corrected by compassion was the best answer.

Roosevelt's genius lay in the fact that he recognized—rather, rejoiced in—the challenge to the pragmatic nerve. His basic principle was not to sacrifice human beings to logic. Frances Perkins describes him as "in full revolt against the 'economic man.'" He had no philosophy save experiment, which was a technique; constitutionalism, which was a procedure; and humanity, which was a faith.

8   FROM   *Irving Bernstein*
The Establishment of Big Labor

Irving Bernstein was a member of Degler's and Schlesinger's generation, and he shared their enthusiasm for the New Deal. Born in Rochester, New York, in 1916 and educated at the University of Rochester and Harvard University, he joined the Institute of Industrial Relations at the University of California at Los Angeles in 1948. He made his first large contribution to New Deal historiography in 1950 with his book The New Deal

SOURCE. Irving Bernstein, *Turbulent Years: A History of the American Worker 1933–1941,* Boston: Houghton Mifflin Co., 1969, pp. 769–779, 786–790. Copyright © 1969 by Irving Bernstein. Reprinted by permission of the publisher, Houghton Mifflin Company.

Collective Bargaining Policy, *and the selection reprinted here
concludes the second volume of his projected three-volume history of the American worker from 1920 to 1941. The eight years
from March 4, 1933, to December 7, 1941, he wrote in the pre-
face to the present volume, "witnessed remarkable and significant changes in the labor movement, in American industry, and
in public policy relating to collective bargaining."*

The most important development that took place was the dramatic increase in the size of the labor movement. If one uses the
National Bureau of Economic Research series, constructed by
Leo Wolman and Leo Troy on conservative criteria, the membership of American unions (excluding Canadian members)
rose from 2,805,000 in 1933 to 8,410,000 in 1941. This constituted an almost exact tripling in size. Perhaps even more significant, for the first time in the history of the nation unions enrolled
a substantial fraction of those at work, by 1941, 23 per cent of
nonagricultural employment. Further, the prospect at the close
of this period was that rapid growth both in absolute numbers
and in the share of employment would continue for at least the
duration of the war.

While expansion was evident in all industry groups, it was
most marked in manufacturing, transportation, and mining. Wolman made the following estimates of the per cent of wage and
salaried employees organized:

	1930	1940
Manufactures	8.8%	34.1%
Transportation, communication, and		
public utilities	23.4	48.2
Building	54.3	65.3
Mining, quarrying, and oil	21.3	72.3
Services	2.7	6.7
Public service	8.3	10.2

Thus, by 1940 those industry groups with heavy concentrations
of blue-collar workers—mining, construction, transportation,

and manufacturing—were highly unionized, and those with predominantly white-collar employment—the services and government—were overwhelmingly unorganized. In effect, the notable advances of the thirties had penetrated deeply into the unorganized sectors of the manual labor force; the gains in the nonmanual areas were slight.

The largest and most significant increases in membership occurred in manufacturing industries. Here it is important to note that manufacturing at that time was by far the biggest of the industry groups, representing more than one third of all nonagricultural employment. Wolman's calculations of the per cent of production workers organized in manufacturers are as follows:

	1930	1941
Metals	10.2%	43.3%
Clothing	47.6	64.4
Food, liquor, and tobacco	11.3	32.5
Paper, printing, and publishing	30.3	41.0
Leather and leather products	12.4	34.0
Chemicals, rubber, clay, glass, and stone	4.7	15.4
Textiles	7.5	14.3
Lumber and woodworking	6.5	11.8

While union membership rose all over the nation, the most notable gains occurred in those regions and states with high concentrations of employment in manufacturing (especially the heavy industries), mining, transportation, and construction. Troy's figures for 1939, the only data available, show the following extent of organization of nonagricultural employment by region:

New England	12.8%
Middle Atlantic	23.5
East North Central	24.2
West North Central	19.1
South Atlantic	13.2
East South Central	16.2
West South Central	10.4
Mountain	19.9
Pacific	27.1

These limited data suggest three levels of regional unionization: high—Pacific, East North Central, and Middle Atlantic; medium —Mountain and West North Central; and low—New England and the three southern regions. It is quite possible that, if statistics were available for 1941, they would show that New England had moved up to the middle group because of penetrations of the textile, shoe, and metalworking industries. While the South, of course, lagged, those states with clusters of employment in mining and heavy manufacturing—Kentucky, Alabama, and Tennessee—were far more highly unionized than the predominantly textile states—North and South Carolina and Georgia.

There can be little doubt that metropolitan influences were much more significant than either state or regional factors. That is, the unionization of a strategic industry concentrated in a major city had a ripple effect, rolling out to smaller communities in which that industry was located, to nearby towns, to other industries in the same metropolitan area. This was evident with the needle trades in New York, with steel in Pittsburgh, with automobiles in Detroit, with rubber in Akron, with trucking in Minneapolis and Seattle, and with the waterfront in San Francisco.

Aside from the growth of membership, the American labor movement during the thirties underwent changes of great significance in both policy and structure.

The issue of industrial unionism, with which the American Federation of Labor had unsuccessfully wrestled since the late nineteenth century, was now substantially resolved by civil war. The craft union theory no longer stood as a bar against industrial organization. The CIO, of course, was firmly dedicated to industrial unionism. Equally significant, by 1941 the AFL had also largely accepted this philosophy as opportunism displaced dogmatism. It is an ironic fact that several of the historic craft unions that fought Lewis so bitterly over this question should now themselves organize on an industrial basis—the Machinists, the Carpenters, the International Brotherhood of Electrical Workers, the Teamsters. While industrial unionism became legitimatized, it did not become supreme. By and large, it set the pattern in the manufacturing and mining industries. But craft unionism retained its dominance in construction, transportation, the services, and the skilled trades. Where the two overlapped, for example, in shipbuilding, in copper mining, among craftsmen in manufacturing, they contested, resorting increasingly to the National Labor Relations Board as the means of resolving conflicts over appropriate unit.

This victory of industrial unionism, joined to the democratic assumption of the Wagner Act, undermined the theory of exclusive jurisdiction, a monopoly concept which taught that an international union's job territory was defined by the charter it received from the Federation. Once gained, title became inviolate. The workers had no right to select another union; the employer might not opt for a rival organization; no other union could legally trespass; the Federation might not withdraw or amend the charter without the holder's consent. While the theory sometimes bowed to the fact of power, this was the accepted doctrine. Since the great majority of charters had been awarded to craft unions, territories were divided up mainly along lines of skill. An industrial organization, by combining several crafts, was a threat to the scheme, almost automatically a "dual" union. The success of the CIO, a combination of industrial unions, shattered the theory of exclusive jurisdiction by creating dual organizations of assured permanency. At the same time the National Labor Relations Act helped to undermine this doctrine. The assumption of the statute was that workers should determine their bargaining agent by secret ballot under the majority rule. They were free to make a selection in defiance of a Federation charter and their choice under law was supreme. While the concept of jurisdiction remained alive in the American labor movement, it could no longer be exclusive. Competition replaced monopoly. In fact, with the passage of time, jurisdictions would become so fouled as to defy any unraveler.

By 1941 dual unionism had become the pattern at most levels of trade-union structure. Nationally the Congress of Industrial Organizations stood opposed to the American Federation of Labor. In many of the states the Industrial Union Councils contested with the State Federations of Labor. More important, in numerous industries international unions affiliated with the CIO were rival to AFL organizations. In coal it was the United Mine Workers v. the Progressive Mine Workers; in automobiles the UAW, CIO v. the UAW, AFL; in aircraft the UAW v. the Machinists; in electrical manufacturing the UE v. the IBEW; in men's clothing the Amalgamated Clothing Workers v. the United Garment Workers; in textiles the Textile Workers' Union v. the United Textile Workers; in lumber the Woodworkers v. the Carpenters; on the waterfront the International Longshoremen's and Warehousemen's Union v. the International Longshoremen's Association; in warehousing the ILWU v. the Teamsters; among seamen the National Maritime Union v. the Seafarers' International Union; in the shipyards the Marine and Shipbuilding Workers v. the Metal Trades; in nonferrous mining Mine, Mill v. the Metal Trades; in meatpacking the Packinghouse Workers v. the Meat Cutters and Butcher Workmen; in transit the Amalgamated Street Railway Employees v. the Transport Workers; in stores the Retail, Wholesale, and Department Store Employees v. the Retail Clerks. And to top everything, Lewis in 1940 launched the Construction Workers' Organizing Committee to challenge the Building Trades.

A consequence of this rival unionism was to spur organizing activity and so the growth of membership. The main impact fell upon the AFL. The CIO, by its defiance and its early dramatic victories, threw down the gauntlet to the Federation. In the late thirties and early forties the AFL affiliates accepted this challenge with a massive commitment to organizing.

By 1941 the AFL had gained a decisive and permanent victory. At the time almost no one either inside or outside the labor movement recognized this significant fact. It was hidden by the mystique of power Lewis had imparted to the CIO, by the highly publicized contemporary successes of SWOC in Little Steel and of the UAW at Ford, and by the deliberate falsification of membership figures. In 1941 the CIO reported its membership as 5 million. According to Troy, its actual membership was 2,654,000. His figure for the AFL is 5,179,000. At the time most people assumed that the two were about the same size. In fact, the AFL was twice as big. Further, the Federation was a sounder organization structurally. It had 106 affiliated international unions, compared to the CIO's 41. These organizations spread across the whole range of industries instead of being confined essentially to manufacturing and mining. The CIO was a lopsided organization with 71 per cent of its membership concentrated in six unions—the UMW, the UAW, SWOC, the Amalgamated Clothing Workers, the UE, and the Textile Workers. Given the bitter mood of John L. Lewis, the CIO could hardly count for long upon the continued affiliation of the largest, richest, and most powerful of these unions. In fact, many of the CIO affiliates were tiny and/or "paper" organizations. Finally, long-term labor force trends, though not widely perceived at the time, favored the AFL. Employment after the war was certain to decline relatively in precisely those areas in which CIO strength gathered—mining and heavy manufacturing. The spread between the rivals would widen with the passage of time. Inevitable AFL dominance would ultimately make a merger possible.

In "Dis What De Union Done," Uncle George said that the UMW had raised the wages of Alabama coal miners. He was indubitably correct. Average weekly earnings in bituminous coal in the nation advanced from $14.47 in 1933 to $30.86 in 1941 and the increase in the mines about Trafford may have been more. But when one moves from the specific to the general, it becomes far more difficult to assess the impact of growing unionism upon the condition of workers. This is because of the great size and diversity of the American economy, the disparity among collective bargaining systems, the subtlety in assigning causes to results, and the inadequacy of the statistics. Despite these impediments, it seems worthwhile to draw a few generalizations, recognizing both that they are not universally applicable and that, in some cases, they are impossible to prove.

There can be no doubt that the rise of unionism in the thirties led to a significant increase in wages. Arthur M. Ross demonstrated this in an analysis of the movement of real hourly earnings between 1933 and 1945 in sixty-five industries grouped by the extent of employment covered by collective bargaining agreements. He found a direct relationship between the per cent of unionization and the per cent of increase in earnings. Thus, union members enjoyed a more rapid rise in wages than nonmembers. Moreover, Ross pointed out, unions also raised the wages of unorganized workers by setting standards of equity for them and their employers and by prodding the latter into granting higher wages in order to keep the union out.

Another wage impact of the new unions, almost certainly, was to narrow differentials in earnings. By comparison with other industrial nations, American differentials were exceptionally wide prior to the Great Depression. The CIO unions in manufacturing industries, in particular, compressed the spread between the skilled and the unskilled by negotiating wage increases across-the-board in cents per hour, rather than per cent. For example, a difference of 100 per cent between an unskilled rate of 50¢ and a skilled rate of $1.00 diminished to 83 per cent when each was pushed up 10¢. Probably this narrowing of skill differentials was relatively modest prior to 1941 because the recession that began in 1937 restrained wage increases for about three years. During the thirties, as well, southern manufacturing industries narrowed historic wage differentials with the North. While unionization was a factor, the NRA codes and the Fair Labor Standards Act of 1938 also contributed to this result.

An important achievement of the new unionism was the introduction of the seniority principle. As might be expected at a time of serious unemployment, seniority was mainly applied to layoffs, transfers, and rehires, and to a lesser extent to promotions. In some industries seniority in layoffs was linked to work-sharing. That is, if the work force must be reduced, the hours of all employees were cut first and thereafter individuals would be laid off in accordance with length of service. One effect of the use of seniority was to restrict management's discretion both in selecting the worker it considered best qualified for the job and in making arbitrary or discriminatory choices. Another was to provide job security for employees with longer service.

Perhaps the most significant accomplishment of the new unions was to establish grievance procedures—what they called industrial democracy and what Sumner H. Slichter named industrial jurisprudence. At the outset this took the form of creating a shop-steward system in the plant and of compelling the employer to deal with it in the disposition of grievances. This led shortly to the erection of hierarchically arranged steps with increased levels of authority on each side through which grievances passed in accordance with time limits. Towards the end of the period a growing but small number of collective bargaining agreements provided for arbitration as the terminal step in the procedure, utilizing an impartial person to render a final and binding award. At the same time the umpire system began to emerge in which a "permanent" arbitrator served on all cases during the life of the agreement. Aside from older arrangements of this sort in the needle trades, hosiery, and anthracite coal, two notable new umpireships were established—in the Pacific Coast longshore industry in 1938 and under the General Motors–AW agreement in 1940. Dean Wayne L. Morse of the University of Oregon Law School served as the West Coast arbitrator, and Professor Harry A. Millis of the University of Chicago was umpire under the General Motors agreement until 1941, when he became chairman of the NLRB. Professor George W. Taylor of the University of Pennsylvania, formerly the impartial chairman under agreements in the full-fashioned hosiery and the Philadelphia men's clothing industries, succeeded him as umpire.

While these procedures for the most part admitted grievances over the whole range of shop issues, their most significant immediate impact was in the area of discipline and discharge. The employer was now required to show cause for taking such action, and the worker who appealed to the grievance procedure was afforded representation and many other elements of due process. Here, again, management's power was narrowed. Workers won protection against arbitrary or discriminatory punishment.

One of the most significant developments of the period was increased political involvement of the American labor movement, the undermining of the historic political neutrality of the American Federation of Labor. Of that earlier posture, V. O. Key, Jr., wrote,

"Over a long period the policies of the American Federation of Labor regarding the role of government were astonishingly similar to those of business. Labor insisted as vociferously as business that the true doctrine was that of *laissez faire:* let the state leave labor alone; it could care for itself through organization, collective bargaining, and the strike. . . .

The political tactics and strategy of the . . . Federation . . . have been designed to fit its politico-economic philosophy. If the principal mode of advancing the cause of labor is through the

strike and collective bargaining, political action will occupy only
a subordinate role. . . . Gompers succeeded in firmly establishing the doctrine that it was inexpedient for labor to attempt to
form an independent political party and seek control of the
government. . . .

Although from time to time the Federation leaders endorse
this or that candidate, the Federation itself cannot and does not
attempt to swing labor as a whole one way or the other."

A number of developments that became manifest in the thirties made this voluntaristic philosophy obsolete. The first was
that American politics, wholly aside from the Great Depression
or the New Deal, was undergoing a profound transformation
with the Democrats supplanting the Relublicans as the majority
party. The Republican Party found its roots among white An-
glo-Saxon Protestants in the business and professional classes in
the cities and, more numerously, in the small towns and on the
farms. But the children of the great pre-1914 "new immigration"
from Southern and Eastern Europe, mainly Catholics and Jews,
who formed much of the urban working class, were now reaching voting age and moving into the Democratic Party. Negro mi-
grants from southern farms to northern cities, dependent upon
federal relief, joined this movement. The influence of the former
had already been evident in their support for Al Smith and the
Democratic Party in the 1928 elections. "When Roosevelt first
took office," Samuel Lubell wrote, "no segment of the population was more ready for 'a new deal' than the submerged, inarti-
culate urban masses." Thus, many members of the new unions
were eager for a more affirmative political policy than that offered by traditional AFL neutrality.

The depression, second, caused urban workers to turn to the
federal government to alleviate their distress, to redress the inequities of the society, and to put the economy back on its feet.
They rejected *laissez faire,* whether of business or of the AFL,
and embraced positive government—relief, unemployment insurance, old age pensions, minimum wages and maximum hours,
and protection of the right to organize and bargain collectively.
"The really revolutionary surge behind the New Deal," Lubell

wrote, "lay in the coupling of the depression with the rise of a new generation."

Third, Roosevelt, who understood this perfectly, made the urban working class the cornerstone of his New Deal–Democratic coalition. He deliberately speeded the process of labor's involvement in politics. National elections now were decided in the industrial states and the workers in the big cities voted overwhelmingly for Democratic candidates headed by the President. A labor movement that remained neutral ran behind its constituents.

John L. Lewis, fourth, who was hardly constrained by AFL traditions, sensed the mood of the workers in the cities and at once committed the CIO to an active political policy of support for Roosevelt, the New Deal, and the Democratic Party. The CIO would never deviate, even when Lewis himself asked it to switch to the Republican candidate in 1940.

Finally, the historic AFL policy best fitted the outlook and needs of the building trades and those unions provided its main support. But in the thirties they declined relatively in power, both among unions as a whole and, at the close of the period, within the Federation. Thus, neutrality became increasingly obsolete as union membership penetrated the non-construction sectors of the labor force.

But tradition dies hard in the labor movement: the AFL would not actually endorse a presidential candidate by name until 1952. Nevertheless, a new political mood was manifest within the Federation in the late thirties. Its deep involvement in the legislative process was abundantly evident at every level of government. Many of its affiliates were as active politically as the CIO and almost invariably in behalf of Roosevelt and the Democratic Party. Dan Tobin of the Teamsters ran the Democratic National Committee's labor program. While William Green was officially neutral, it was hardly a secret that he supported Roosevelt enthusiastically. In fact, Big Bill Hutcheson's most notable public claim to fame at the time was that he was the only prominent Republican left in the labor movement. By the end of the period, therefore, both union leadership and union membership were politically involved, overwhelmingly committed to Franklin Roosevelt, to his New Deal programs, and to the Democratic Party.

It was more than happenstance that the great cases that tested the validity of the Wagner Act should lie at the center of the consitutional crisis of 1937. This was because the period witnessed a change in American law so profound as to constitute a revolution. Most of the principles that received statutory and judicial expression in the thirties, to be sure, had roots extending back to an earlier period, in some cases deep into the nineteenth century. But there were two characteristics of public policy in the New Deal era that distinguished it fundamentally from these antecedents.

The first was comprehensive and permanent regulation by government. The National Labor Relations Act and the Railway Labor Act did more than establish rules to control the initiation and conduct of collective bargaining; these statutes also set up administrative agencies to enforce these rules. Several of the states followed the federal example by passing "little" Wagner Acts and by creating "little" Labor Boards.

The second was a fundamental shift in the posture of public policy on collective bargaining from neutrality to affirmation. Earlier, government, by its statutory silence, assumed that the contest between labor and management was an essentially private matter. While it was lawful for workers to organize and bargain collectively, as William M. Leiserson wrote, "the law recognized the equal freedom of the employers to destroy labor organizations and to deny the right of employees to join trade unions." The courts took an impartial position, notably by applying the Sherman Act's proscription against contracts, combinations, and conspiracies in restraint of trade to unions as well as to corporations. A legal system under which government played a neutral role had the effect of tipping the balance of bargaining power in most American industries in favor of employers. The turn to affirmation found most dramatic expression in Section 1 of the Wagner Act. This premise of the statute asserted that "inequality of bargaining power between employees who do not possess full freedom of association or actual liberty of contract, and employers who are organized in the corporate or other forms of ownership association" burdened commerce, aggravated depressions, reduced wages, and depressed the purchasing power of wage earners. Thus, it now became "the policy of the United

States" to remove obstructions to commerce "by encouraging the practice and procedure of collective bargaining." The courts joined in the movement to affirmation, especially by removing unions from the reach of the Sherman Act insofar as they engaged in bargaining functions, and by treating peaceful picketing as a protected form of freedom of speech under the First Amendment.

While responsive to the needs of a troubled industrial society, this basic change in public policy had qualities of a historical accident insofar as the Wagner Act was concerned. It is entirely possible, perhaps probable, that no Congress in modern American history except the 74th could have mustered majorities for such a bill in both the House and the Senate. The usual combination of Republicans and Southern Democrats would have prevented this. Yet the measure was brought in at the precise rare moment when it could be passed. Further, the National Labor Relations bill was in no sense an Administration proposal. President Roosevelt, in fact, showed little interest in and less support for Senator Wagner's bill until the penultimate stage when the Supreme Court, by nullifying NRA, left him no option. It seemed almost as though the nation had stumbled into a basic change in policy.

This governmental commitment to collective bargaining would lead to a number of significant consequences. The first was to spur the growth of union membership. There were, of course, other reasons to help explain the expansion of membership—an improved economic climate, the CIO campaigns in the mass-production industries, the AFL response to rival unionism. But the law laid the legal foundation. The National Labor Relations Act and the Railway Labor Act served both as a stimulus to organization and as a shield against interference by employers with its achievement.

Second, belligerent antiunion practices of employers substantially disappeared from American industrial relations. Within a few years of the passage of the Wagner Act such devices as industrial espionage, professional strikebreaking, antiunion private police, industrial munitioning, and company-dominated unions fell into disuse and the incidence of discrimination against and discharge for union membership was significantly reduced. This was a great victory for civil liberties in the shop. As against the employer, the law now guaranteed to the worker freedom of speech, freedom of assembly, and freedom of association. It also sharply reduced the level of violence in American industry, a notable gain in a society with a high propensity towards the use of force.

A third result was to diminish the need for and the incidence of the most difficult form of strike, that over union recognition. The representation machinery of the National Labor Relations Board and the National Mediation Board became a substitute for the work stoppage over organization; the peaceful election was the alternative to a test of economic power. While many employers in the early years declined to accept these representation procedures, after 1939 compliance improved and the relative number of strikes over recognition declined.

Another impact, fourth, was to undermine the appeal of Marxism, particularly of the Communist Party, to American workers. It was the realization of the prediction of such supporters of the Wagner bill in 1935 as Lloyd Garrison and Harry Millis, in the words of the former, "the safety measure" theory. This worked out in two ways. The more important was to strengthen a labor movement overwhelmingly committed to business unionism by increasing the volume of its business—collective bargaining. The second was to show that one of the fundamental tenets of Marxism, that the state under capitalism must serve as the instrument of the ruling class, was incorrect.

A fifth consequence was to strengthen industrial democracy, broadly defined. The representation election itself was a demonstration of the democratic process at work. Civil liberties were now legally underwritten in industry. More significant still, collective bargaining, particularly the grievance procedure, compelled the employer to share information and power in the decision-making process in the shop. In Milton Derber's terms, "unilateral control" gave way to "bilateralism."

Sixth, government regulation led inevitably to the "legalization" of collective bargaining; that is, the lawyers made a grand entrance. The quasi-judicial character of the Labor Board and the frequency of appeals to the courts made their services necessary. Insecure employers who could afford the luxury also brought them into negotiations and into arbitrations, and unions increasingly followed this example. The law schools introduced the systematic teaching of labor relations law; the law journals filled their pages with labor articles; commercial services published Board and court decisions; a specialized bar emerged, one part serving employers and the other unions; collective bargaining agreements, reflecting the lawyer's influence and style, became longer, more formal, more involved, more guarded in language; some arbitrators, notably Wayne Morse, "judicialized" the arbitration process.

A seventh result of federal intervention was to give the CIO a short-run advantage in its struggle with the AFL. This was because the CIO unions grasped more quickly than many of their more hidebound AFL rivals the gains to be made by employing the Board's machinery, because the early NLRB showed some favoritism to the CIO, and because the Wagner Act helped to undermine the principle of exclusive jurisdiction. But this edge wore off after a few years when the AFL affiliates learned to use the Board, when Leiserson replaced Donald Wakefield Smith and Millis supplanted Warren Madden, and when exclusive jurisdiction lost much of its relevancy. By the time of Pearl Harbor, if not a year or two earlier, the CIO and the AFL stood equal before the government.

Eighth, the federal commitment to the regulation of collective bargaining was to prove permanent. The Wagner Act, viewed as an exercise in American politics, concluded the era of neutrality. That statute, reflecting the pro-labor sentiment of the 74th Congress, confined regulation to the conduct of employers. But, given the assurance of some future swing in the political pendulum, already evident in some of the states, the legislature would certainly amend the law to restrict unions, both in the bargaining process and in the conduct of their internal affairs.

This was because, finally, American employers, though by 1941 coming into substantial compliance, refused to accept the law as the final word. They were determined to turn the statute against unions and to overhaul the "G __ __ D __ __ __ Labor Board."

9 FROM   *Clarke A. Chambers*
The Implementation of Postwar Progressivism

*Another contemporary of Degler and Schlesinger, Clarke A.
Chambers also developed a positive interpretation of modern
American reform. Born in Blue Earth, Minnesota, in 1921, he
was educated at Carleton College and the University of California, Berkeley, and became a member of the history department
at the University of Minnesota. He defined himself as "the child
of the 1930's and the New Deal" and "a participant in the work
of the Christian Social Relations Commission of my home par-
ish, a member of the Urban League, and a precinct worker for
Minnesota's Democratic senators," Hubert Humphrey and Eugene McCarthy. He represented, in other words, the large influence of liberalism on New Deal historiography in the late 1950's
and early 1960's.*

*While Chamber's first book-length contribution to New Deal
historiography dealt with farm politics, focusing on California's
farm organizations, his second was concerned with urban groups
—social workers and social reformers in voluntary reform associations and social service agencies—and sought to provide a
partial answer to the question of what happened to the reform
impulse between the New Nationalism and the New Freedom, on
the one hand, and the New Deal on the other. "Students of
American liberalism," he wrote, "have traditionally treated the
Great War as the end of reform and the decade between armistice and panic as a great hiatus; historians, concerned with the
continuity of reform, have tended to discount the decade of 'normalcy and reaction,' and to leapfrog over it, often clumsily, from*

SOURCE. Clarke A. Chambers, *Seedtime of Reform: American Social Service
and Social Action 1918–1933,* Minneapolis: University of Minnesota Press,
1963, pp. 26, 82–83, 226, 253–254, 256–258, 265–267. Copyright © 1963 by the
University of Minnesota Press. Reprinted by permission of the publisher.

the backs of T.R. and Woodrow Wilson to the back of F.D.R."
Chambers and others in the late 1950's and the 1960's chal-
lenged this interpretation and suggested that developments in the
1920's prepared Americans to change their economic system in
certain ways in the following decade. Without those prepara-
tions, he assumes, the history of the 1930's would have been sig-
nificantly different from what it was. He also assumes, it appears,
that history moves in stages, in a step-by-step, evolutionary fashion,
and that modern American reform is significant and valuable. It
has improved American life.

We have fallen too easily into the generalization that the decade from armistice to panic was marked by one prolonged and
uninterrupted slump in reform thought and determination, when
the processes were more subtle and more complicated than that.
Through frustration there persisted an unending search for new
ways to meet problems both old and new when old ways fell
short or (as was as often the case) when perfectly reasonable
means of legislative action were overruled by hostile judicial rul-
ings.

Particularly in the actions of voluntary associations dedicated
to reform causes was the field never surrendered to the forces of
reaction. Beleaguered and beaten back, these social-reform
movements recruited new leaders and enlisted new soldiers,
somehow scraped up the money to keep at least a token force
well armed, experimented with new field tactics and in time
evolved new strategies.

A small band, a Gideon's army, kept the faith, working
through little voluntary associations, operating on a shoestring.
Up and down the country they wandered, lecturing, writing,
studying, exhorting. They converged on city councils, on state
assemblies, and on Congress to testify and to witness to their be-
liefs. Rebuffed, reviled, ridiculed, they kept the faith. Turned
back again and again, they began to pioneer new methods and
post new goals. Out of defeat was born the desire to seek out new
paths of reform, new roads to Zion. Out of frustration was born

social imagination. By the end of the decade, new devices for social reconstruction, devices that anticipated much of the central
program of the New Deal, had been elaborated.

An understanding of where progressivism led and an appre-
ciation of whence the New Deal derived require study of reform
associations and movements in these years. In voluntary action
progressivism survived in the decade of normalcy and reaction,
even if it did not triumph. In the National Consumers' League
and the Women's Trade Union League, in the National Child
Labor Committee, the Association for Old Age Security, the
American Association for Labor Legislation, and the League of
Women Voters, the reform impulse was kept alive. In the arena
of professional social work, in the Child Welfare League and the
National Federation of Settlements, in the National Conference
of Social Work and the American Association of Social Workers,
new ways of social amelioration and of social action were being
pioneered. In many cases the leaders were directly out of prewar
progressivism—Jane Addams, Lillian Wald, Graham Taylor,
John L. Elliott, Lillie Peck, Mary Simkhovitch, John B. and
Irene O. Andrews, Florence Kelley, Owen Lovejoy, Samuel Mc-
Cune Lindsay, Margaret Dreier Robins, Paul Kellogg. Other
leaders had been fed on progressivism, but did not really come
into their own until the interwar era—John R. Commons, Bruno
Lasker, Abraham Epstein, Edward Clopper, Elisabeth Christ-
man, Felix Frankfurter, Isaac Rubinow, Gertrude Vaile, Eduard
Lindeman, Porter R. Lee. Still others were relative newcomers
on their way to positions of much greater influence in the
1930's: Mary Dewson, Paul Douglas, Harry Hopkins, Frances
Perkins, Aubrey Williams, Helen Hall, Helen Alfred, Edwin E.
Witte, Arthur J. Altmeyer, Hilda Smith, Mary Anderson, Jacob
Billikopf, Harry Lurie, Jane Hoey, and a host of others whose
names have recurred in this narrative. Rooted in progressivism
and on their way (unwittingly) to the New Deal, social reformers and social servants evidenced a remarkable vitality and imagination during the years that lay between the armistice and the
inauguration of Franklin Roosevelt.

Over and over the point was hammered home—industrial
minima were required not alone as humanitarian considerations
or as charity but as measures essential to the over-all long-run

efficiency of industry, to community health and welfare, and to social stability and orderly progress. The New York Consumers' League offered as its slogan for 1927 "Social Justice Is the Best Safeguard against Social Disorder"; while Florence Kelley, commenting on the violent textile strikes of 1929, insisted that the only alternative to industrial disorder and social strife was "peaceful progress" through legislation.

It was perhaps Newton Baker who best summarized the need for social action to remedy the grievances associated with intense industrialization. Given the growing impersonality of all society, the sanctions of civilization were not as easily applied as once they were. The role of voluntary associations, such as the Consumers' League, was to "investigate, record, agitate" in order that men of good will might act with the knowledge of the consequences of their behavior, while the law coerced the "recalcitrants." The league and its allies could show the way for society to accomplish "on a large and collective scale, in a collective way, that which we so delighted to do as individuals under simpler conditions."

The New Deal drew heavily and specifically upon these concepts, which had grown out of progressivism and had been tempered in the 1920's. The depression afforded the occasion for their implementation, because economic crisis overrode most other considerations in 1933. The National Recovery Administration prohibited child labor, and encouraged codes of labor standards governing hours, wages, and conditions for both women and men workers. When the NRA was broken, the industrial minima were rewritten in the Fair Labor Standards Act of 1938; and this time the Supreme Court concurred. The contribution of liberal reform in the 1920's had been to keep alive the progressive objectives, and then to modify them, extend them, and elaborate a rationale which, under the pressure of emergency, was incorporated as part of the New Deal consensus and program.

The day of harvest was at hand. Before the forward surge of reform ran into domestic opposition, 1937–1938, and dwindled away as the nation passed from peace to war again, many bits of unfinished business left over from the Progressive Era and many items on the reform agenda during the postwar years had been taken care of. Child labor was outlawed in the blanket codes of the National Recovery Administration, and when the NRA was found to be unconstitutional, Grace Abbott, Katharine Lenroot, and the National Child Labor Committee's lobby saw to the inclusion of its prohibition in the Fair Labor Standards Act of 1938. The hours and wages of all workers engaged in interstate commerce came under regulation in 1938; and if the standards were modest and the exemptions broad, millions received wage increases and in time, as amendments were added, the standards were raised and the exemptions narrowed. The federal government initiated programs of slum clearance and public housing which, if they never fully realized the hopes of Helen Alfred and Mary Simkhovitch and other agitators for housing reform, did represent first steps at least. Except for the omission of health insurance the federal social security program enacted in 1935 realized just about all the reformers' hopes, even though Abraham Epstein and some others were disappointed that the act did not go far enough or invariably provide the best administrative procedures. To unemployment and old-age insurance were added federal assistance for the dependent aged, for dependent children, for the blind, for maternal and infant health programs. The Federal Emergency Relief Administration, the Civil Works Administration, the Civilian Conservation Corps, and the Works Progress Administration together provided direct cash relief for the unemployed and wherever possible work relief on constructive projects. The Public Works Administration implemented the design for the long-range planning of major construction projects. The Tennessee Valley Authority provided coordinated plans for the manufacture of electric power and fertilizer, flood control, navigation improvement, soil conservation and reforestation, and recreational facilities. To all these programs reform associations and leaders made immeasurable contributions.

The roll call of prominent New Dealers (and of equal significance, hundreds of lesser public servants who packed New Deal administrations) includes the names of many who were either actively engaged in reform and welfare associations or directly moved by their agitation. Frances Perkins and Harry Hopkins lead the list, of course. Not far behind is Mary (Molly) Dewson, whose career carried straight through from progressivism to the New Deal without interruption. Educated at Wellesley College,

Miss Dewson went directly from the classroom to investigations of the working conditions of women workers in factories and shops for the Women's Education and Industrial Union in Boston. In 1900 she became superintendent of the Parole Department for Girls of the Massachusetts Industrial School at Lancaster. Before enlisting in the woman-suffrage crusade, in 1911, she served briefly as secretary of the Massachusetts Commission on Minimum Wage Legislation. After a tour of duty with the Red Cross in France she became a research director for the National Consumers' League in which capacity she amassed the factual evidence that Felix Frankfurter employed in the *Adkins* case, after which she moved to New York where she served first as civic secretary of the New York Women's City Club and then as president of the New York Consumers' League, from 1927 to 1932.

With Eleanor Roosevelt she campaigned for Al Smith in 1928, headed the Women's Division of the Democratic party in 1932, organized the quietly effective campaign to put across Frances Perkins as secretary of labor, served on the Advisory Council to the President's Committee on Social Security, and became a member of the Social Security Board in 1937. During Roosevelt's first administration she saw that women received at least some share in patronage. She concentrated her efforts on the use of political procedures for the winning of substantive results. From long association with Florence Kelley she had learned the value in bringing to bear upon one issue at a time all the energy one could muster, and the necessity for sound research and broad publicity before moving into action.

Many others were in government long before 1933, and had labored on board and commission for welfare programs that won more generous backing beginning with the New Deal years. Julia Lathrop, Grace Abbott, Katharine Lenroot of the Children's Bureau, Mary Van Kleeck, Mary N. Winslow, and Mary Anderson in the Women's Bureau maintained the closest working relationships with the Consumers' League, the Women's Trade Union League, and the League of Women Voters, and with friends in settlement and social work throughout their long careers. The lines of influence, in these cases, worked both ways, from voluntary associations to public service and back.

To the task of drawing plans for comprehensive social security Roosevelt called those he knew had been working with the infinitely intricate problems of insurance for many years. Witte and Altmeyer came with backgrounds of more than a decade's pioneering in Wisconsin on unemployment compensation and related programs. Business and labor were represented on the Advisory Council to the President's Committee on Economic Security; among those who had been active in social reform movements were Paul Kellogg, editor of the *Survey* magazine; Belle Sherwin, former president of the National League of Women Voters; Grace Abbott of the Children's Bureau; George H. Nordlen of the Fraternal Order of Eagles; Josephine Roche, business woman, public servant, and member of the Consumers' League; and Mary Dewson. On Paul Kellogg's urging, Helen Hall and Joel D. Hunter, the latter general superintendent of the United Charities of Chicago, were added to the council; at Witte's suggesion, after it was noted that no Catholic had been named, Roosevelt appointed John A. Ryan. Acting in a technical advisory capacity were such social insurance pioneers and experts as William R. Leiserson, Murray W. Latimer, Aubrey Williams, Bryce Stewart, Barbara N. Armstrong, Meredith B. Givers, Eveline Burns, Ewan Clague, Grace Abbott, Katharine Lenroot, and many others. Neither Abraham Epstein nor Isaac Rubinow was formally involved in the deliberation, the latter because of ill health.

The gross sense of insecurity that accompanied the depression undoubtedly created a climate favorable to social security legislation; the political threat of the Townsend movement made action on old-age security eminently expedient; the determination of F. D. R. and of Frances Perkins to give social security one of the highest priorities brought imaginative leadership to its accomplishment. Two additional vital factors were present: the existence of a small group of experts, learned and experienced, to give shape and substance to the act; and the momentum of agitation that reformers and welfare leaders supplied. Without the pioneer studies and propaganda of Epstein, Rubinow, Andrews, Commons, and Douglas would the nation have been prepared for social security in 1935? The experts provided the requisite technical knowledge and contributed to a favorable environment, in which there was readiness to accept a principle and a program that western Europe and nations of the Commonwealth had inaugurated many years earlier.

Before an overflow audience of social workers at their national conference in June 1933, Harry Hopkins brought the word they had been waiting to hear. Everyone was expected to pitch in and do the best he could to provide relief; certainly the federal government was eager to experiment, and if some of the expedients did not work, well, "the world will not come to an end." The need for action was urgent: "We propose to see that the unemployed get some relief." With equal bluntness he announced to the American Public Welfare Association, a year later when the desperate emergency had passed, that the need was now for "regular and orderly assistance"—pensions for the aged without regard to need, widows' pensions, special provisions for the unemployable. Compulsory health insurance was desirable, so was the planning of public works—parks, forests, roads, housing. In all these programs—which aimed at security, the good life, freedom from fear—social workers had been leading the way for years. Looking back upon eight years of New Deal experience, Jane Hoey, who had done as much as anyone within the ranks of federal government to develop its programs of public assistance, proclaimed that the New Deal carried through principles for which social workers had labored—the dependence of political democracy upon social and economic democracy; "the assumption by government of a continuing responsibility for promoting the general welfare"; the provision of "regular income" for all families through private employment, public work, social insurance, and public assistance. In the administration of public assistance programs the New Deal had accepted the social workers' insistence upon fair hearings, "unrestricted and unconditional cash payments," and the confidential nature of all records.

It is understandable that those who had labored in the dry seasons rejoiced when reforms, long-agitated, came into their own in the fullness of time. Julia Lathrop and Florence Kelley died in 1932, before they could see the harvest of their recent efforts. But Lillian Wald, testifying in 1935 that she was "very much for

Roosevelt," expressed gratification that many reform goals were being fulfilled that she had feared would be such a long time coming.

The calendar of events may be recorded briefly: The 8th of June 1934: In a special message to Congress, the President—privately dedicated to security for all Americans "from the cradle to the grave," impelled now by a rising popular demand for action (of which the Townsend movement was most vociferous), confronted with congressional initiative (the Dill-Connery old-age bill, the Wagner-Lewis unemployment insurance bill)—called for a broad program of security, "the security of the home, the security of livelihood, and the security of social insurance." The 29th of June 1934: By Executive Order the Committee on Economic Security was called into existence. The 26th of July 1934: Edwin E. Witte, chief of the Wisconsin Legislative Reference Library since 1922, arrived in Washington to take up his post as executive director of the committee. The 21st of January 1935: The committee's omnibus draft bill went to Congress for committee hearings. The 14th of August 1935: congressional redrafting and passage of the bill having been accomplished, the President signed that act which Frances Perkins later reported gave him greater satisfaction than any other domestic accomplishment. It provided a federal-state system of unemployment insurance; a federal program of old-age insurance; federal grants to the states for old-age assistance, aid to the blind, aid to dependent children, aid to maternal and child-health services, aid to child-welfare services, and aid to public health programs. Before the bill was finally enacted, limitations and exemptions had been added, but only health and invalidism insurance was totally excluded, this against the wishes of Miss Perkins and Harry Hopkins but in accord with the dictates of political expediency, the fear that its inclusion would have placed the entire program in jeopardy.

What was true for social security was true for other reform measures as well. Provision of direct federal aid for unemployment relief; an expressed preference for work relief whenever possible with payment in cash and without casework supervision of family budgets; support of public works; guarantees of the right of labor to organize and bargain collectively; the prohibition of child labor; statutory provision for maximum hours and minimum wages—these were the fruits of crisis politics and the leadership of a President eager to act in an emergency greater than war; they were the fruits of tireless study and propaganda by reformers and reform associations who had hotly contested the issues of social justice while the nation kept cool with Coolidge.

With the inauguration of Roosevelt, in the depths of the depression, the opportunity for reconstructive measures presented itself. While the New Deal never offered fully valid solutions to the economic problem of depression (as the persistence of mass unemployment attests), it did initiate measures that provided built-in stabilizers of substantial efficacy, and it did afford a larger measure of social justice and a more equitable distribution of income and social power than the previous generation had known. If progressivism, from which it drew inspiration, was more hardheaded than many historians have recorded, the New Deal was laced more heavily with moral purpose than most critics believed. From progressivism and from reform movements in the post-war decade it drew both its methods of analysis and its spiritual inspiration.

The New Deal was eclectic in both theory and program. It provided no logically consistent, perfectly coherent, formal system of social thought. What Clinton Rossiter has written of the political theory of the Revolutionary generation might well apply, on a lower level of brilliance one fears, to the consensus of the 1930's. The leaders of the American Revolution, he writes, were "makers of history with a flair for speculative generalization, not philosophers in single minded search of ultimate truth." The philosophy they pieced together was "earnest faith rather than ordered theory." Its genius was evident in its capacity to fashion real institutions for the implementation of popular ideas. Hyde Park was not Monticello, to be sure; yet the similarities cannot be denied.

Out of pressing need the New Deal evolved a program; from the past it drew its inspiration. The inventiveness of the New Deal operated more in the arena of program than abstract policy. That it was not devoid of lively and viable theories, however, is abundantly clear. It succeeded, where it did succeed, not only because it was administered by clever politicians, not only because it proposed real, if always partial, answers to real and present problems; it succeeded also because its idiom drew from a tradition still revered in the American heart. It owed a profound debt to those reform and welfare leaders who had pioneered new programs and kept alive the tradition of humane liberalism in the years of normalcy.

Grace Abbott was right, it was uphill all the way; yes, to the very end. And it did offer great rewards, not only to those who enlisted in the long, hard struggle, but to the whole nation as well.

10   FROM   *Ellis W. Hawley*
The Survival of Big Business

Ellis Hawley represents the rise of a new and more critical generation in New Deal historiography. He had known the depression and the New Deal firsthand but only as a very young boy and had come of age after the New Deal was an established part of American life. Born in Cambridge, Kansas, in 1929, he was educated at the University of Wichita, Kansas University, and the University of Wisconsin. In Lawrence, James C. Malin, a critic of the large influence of liberalism on the historical profession and of the New Deal, aroused Hawley's interest in the New Deal's business policies and perhaps nourished his scepticism about them, and in Madison, Howard K. Beale, Robert A. Lively, and Paul F. Sharp helped him develop the interest that resulted in his first book, from which the following selection was taken and which was published while Hawley was teaching at North Texas State University. (He is now on the faculty of the State University of Iowa.) Earlier writers, such as Mitchell, had

SOURCE. Ellis W. Hawley, *The New Deal and the Problem of Monopoly: A Study in Economic Ambivalence*, pp. vii–viii, 14–16, 476–490 (with deletions). Copyright © 1969 by Princeton University Press; Princeton Paperback, 1969. Reprinted by permission of Princeton University Press.

called attention to the intellectual confusion within the New Deal, but Hawley developed this theme much more fully. And he noted that it was not a problem peculiar to New Dealers but was a significant part of American culture and American history. He assumed that a political leader could not free himself from the confusion, commit himself to one policy, and pursue it consistently. If the situation did not prevent change, it did block revolution.

One of the central problems of twentieth-century America has revolved about the difficulty of reconciling a modern industrial order, necessarily based upon a high degree of collective organization, with democratic postulates, competitive ideals, and liberal individualistic traditions inherited from the nineteenth century. This industrial order has created in America a vision of material abundance, a dream of abolishing poverty and achieving economic security for all; and the great majority of Americans have not been willing to destroy it lest that dream be lost. Yet at the same time it has involved, probably necessarily, a concentration of economic power, a development of monopolistic arrangements, and a loss of individual freedom and initiative, all of which run counter to inherited traditions and ideals. Americans, moreover, have never really decided what to do about this industrial order. Periodically they have debated the merits of "regulated competition" and "regulated monopoly," of trustbusting and economic planning; and periodically they have embarked upon reform programs that would remake the economic system. Yet the resulting reforms have been inconsistent and contradictory. Policies that would promote competition have been interspersed with those that would limit or destroy it. And American economists as a whole have never reached any real consensus in regard to the origins and nature of monopoly, its effects, or the methods of dealing with it.

During the period covered by this study, the six-year span from 1933 to 1939, this conflict over economic policy was particularly acute. The industrial machine, for all its productivity, was seemingly unable to fulfill the dream of abundance and security, and its failure to do so led to demands for political action. Yet there was little agreement on the course that this action should take. Did the situation call for centralized planning and detailed regulation? Did it call for a restoration of competition? Or did it call for government-sponsored cartels that could rationalize the competitive process and weather deflationary forces? In practice, there were a variety of pressures and forces pushing the government in all of these directions. The result was an amalgam of conflicting policies and programs, one that might make some sense to the politician, but little to a rational economist.

Under depression conditions, this clash of values and policies became particularly acute. On the one hand, the depression produced insistent demands for planning, rationalization, and the erection of market controls that could stem the forces of deflation and prevent economic ruin. On the other, it intensified antimonopoly sentiment, destroyed confidence in business leadership, and produced equally insistent demands that big business be punished and competitive ideals be made good. The dilemma of the New Deal reform movement lay in the political necessity of meeting both sets of these demands, in the necessity of creating organizations and controls that could check deflationary forces and provide a measure of order and security while at the same time preserving democratic values, providing the necessary incentives, and making the proper concessions to competitive symbols. From a political standpoint, the Roosevelt Administration could ignore neither of these conflicting currents of pressure and opinion; and under the circumstances, it could hardly be expected to come up with an intellectually coherent and logically consistent set of business policies.

From the viewpoint of a logical economist, about the only term that could adequately describe these conflicting policies and gyrations would be "economic confusion." The New Deal began with government sponsorship of cartels and business planning; it ended with the antitrust campaign and the attack on rigid prices; and along the way, it engaged in minor excursions into socialism, public utility regulation, and the establishment of "government yardsticks." Certainly, there was little in the way of economic consistency. Nor was there much success in terms of restoring prosperity and full employment. Neither the planning approach nor antitrust action nor any of the compromises in between ever contributed much to economic recovery, although they did lead to increased governmental activities of each sort. Recovery, when it came, was largely a product of large-scale government spending, and not of any major reorganization of the business system.

From a political standpoint, however, there was a certain amount of consistency and logic to the New Deal programs. In dealing with business, Roosevelt faced a political dilemma. On the one hand he was confronted with strong pressures for punitive action against big business and with the necessity of making proper obeisance to the antitrust tradition. On the other was the growing pressure for some sort of planning, control, and rationalization. As a practical matter, his Administration did a fairly respectable job of satisfying both sets of demands. The denunciations of "monopoly" and the attack on unpopular groups like Wall Street, the Power Trust, and the Sixty Families kept the antitrusters happy, while at the same time organized industrial pressure groups were being allowed to write their programs of market control into law, particularly in areas where they could come up with the necessary lobbies and symbols. Politically speaking, New Deal business policy was a going concern, and one of the basic tasks of this book is to explain why this was so and how this policy developed and changed.

To condemn these policies for their inconsistencies was to miss the point. From an economic standpoint, condemnation might very well be to the point. They were inconsistent. One line of action tended to cancel the other, with the result that little was accomplished. Yet from the political standpoint, this very inconsistency, so long as the dilemma persisted, was the safest method of retaining political power. President Roosevelt, it seems, never suffered politically from his reluctance to choose between planning and antitrust action. His mixed emotions so closely reflected the popular mind that they were a political asset rather than a liability.

That New Deal policy was inconsistent, then, should occasion little surprise. Such inconsistency, in fact, was readily apparent in the National Industrial Recovery Act, the first major effort to deal with the problems of industrial organization. When Roosevelt took office in 1933, the depression had reached its most acute stage. Almost every economic group was crying for salvation through political means, for some sort of rationalization and planning, although they might differ as to just who was to do the planning and the type and amount of it that would be required. Pro-business planners, drawing upon the trade association ideology of the nineteen twenties and the precedent of the War Industries Board, envisioned a semi-cartelized business commonwealth in which industrial leaders would plan and the state would enforce the decisions. Other men, convinced that there was already too much planning by businessmen, hoped to create an order in which other economic groups would participate in the policy-making process. Even under these circumstances, however, the resulting legislation had to be clothed in competitive symbols. Proponents of the NRA advanced the theory that it would help small businessmen and industrial laborers by protecting them from predatory practices and monopolistic abuses. The devices used to erect monopolistic controls became "codes of fair competition." And each such device contained the proper incantation against monopoly.

Consequently, the NRA was not a single program with a single objective, but rather a series of programs with a series of objectives, some of which were in direct conflict with each other. In effect, the National Industrial Recovery Act provided a phraseology that could be used to urge almost any approach to the problem of economic organization and an administrative machine that each of the conflicting economic and ideological groups might possibly use for their own ends. Under the circumstances, a bitter clash over basic policies was probably inevitable.

For a short period these inconsistencies were glossed over by the summer boomlet of 1933 and by a massive propaganda campaign appealing to wartime precedents and attempting to create a new set of cooperative symbols. As the propaganda wore off, however, and the economic indices turned downward again, the inconsistencies inherent in the program moved to the forefront of the picture. In the code-writing process, organized business had emerged as the dominant economic group, and once this became apparent, criticism of the NRA began to mount. Agrarians, convinced that rising industrial prices were canceling out any gains from the farm program, demanded that businessmen live up to the competitive faith. Labor spokesmen, bitterly disillusioned when the program failed to guarantee union recognition and collective bargaining, charged that the Administration had sold out to management. Small businessmen, certain that the new code authorities were only devices to increase the power of their larger rivals, raised the ancient cry of monopolistic exploitation. Antitrusters, convinced that the talk about strengthening competition was sheer hypocrisy, demanded that this disastrous trust-building program come to a halt. Economic planners, alienated by a process in which the businessmen did the planning, charged that the government was only sanctioning private monopolistic arrangements. And the American public, disillusioned with rising prices and the failure of the program to bring economic recovery, listened to the criticisms and demanded that its competitive ideals be made good.

The rising tide of public resentment greatly strengthened the hand of those that viewed the NRA primarily as a device for raising the plane of competition and securing social justice for labor. Picking up support from discontented groups, from other governmental agencies, and from such investigations as that conducted by Clarence Darrow's National Recovery Review Board, this group within the NRA had soon launched a campaign to bring about a reorientation in policy. By June 1934 it had obtained a formal written policy embodying its views, one that committed the NRA to the competitive ideal, renounced the use of price and production controls, and promised to subject the code authorities to strict public supervision. By this time however, most of the major codes had been written, and the market restorers were never able to apply their policy to codes already approved. The chief effect of their efforts to do so was to antagonize businessmen and to complicate the difficulties of enforcing code provisions that were out of line with announced policy.

The result was a deadlock that persisted for the remainder of the agency's life. Putting the announced policy into effect would have meant, in all probability, the complete alienation of business support and the collapse of the whole structure. Yet accepting and enforcing the codes for what they were would have resulted, again in all probability, in an outraged public and congressional opinion that would have swept away the whole edifice. Thus the NRA tended to reflect the whole dilemma confronting the New Deal. Admittedly, declared policy was inconsistent with practice. Admittedly, the NRA was accomplishing little. Yet from a political standpoint, if the agency were to continue at all, a deadlock of this sort seemed to be the only solution. If the Supreme Court had not taken a hand in the matter, the probable outcome would have been either the abolition of the agency or a continuation of the deadlock.

The practical effect of the NRA, then, was to allow the erection, extension, and fortification of private monopolistic arrangements, particularly for groups that already possessed a fairly high degree of integration and monopoly power. Once these arrangements had been approved and vested interests had developed, the Administration found it difficult to deal with them. It could not move against them without alienating powerful interest groups, producing new economic dislocations, and running the risk of setting off the whole process of deflation again. Yet, because of the competitive ideal, it could not lend much support to the arrangements or provide much in the way of public supervision. Only in areas where other arguments, other ideals, and political pressure justified making an exception, in such areas as agriculture, natural resources, transportation, and to a certain extent labor, could the government lend its open support and direction.

Moreover, the policy dilemma, coupled with the sheer complexity of the undertaking, made it impossible to provide much central direction. There was little planning of a broad, general nature, either by businessmen or by the state; there was merely the half-hearted acceptance of a series of legalized, but generally uncoordinated, monopolistic combinations. The result was not over-all direction, but a type of partial, piecemeal, pressure-group planning, a type of planning designed by specific economic groups to balance production with consumption regardless of the dislocations produced elsewhere in the economy.

There were, certainly, proposals for other types of planning. But under the circumstances, they were and remained politically unfeasible, both during the NRA period and after. The idea of a government-supported business commonwealth still persisted, and a few men still felt that if the NRA had really applied it, the depression would have been over. Yet in the political context of the time, the idea was thoroughly unrealistic. For one thing, there was the growing gap between businessmen and New Dealers, the conviction of one side that cooperation would lead to bureaucratic socialism, of the other that it would lead to fascism or economic oppression. Even if this quarrel had not existed, the Administration could not have secured a program that ran directly counter to the anti-big-business sentiment of the time. The monopolistic implications in such a program were too obvious, and there was little that could be done to disguise them. Most industrial leaders recognized the situation, and the majority of them came to the conclusion that a political program of this sort was no longer necessary. With the crisis past and the deflationary process checked, private controls and such governmental aids as tariffs, subsidies, and loans would be sufficient.

The idea of national economic planning also persisted. A number of New Dealers continued to advocate the transfer of monopoly power from businessmen to the state or to other organized economic groups. Each major economic group, they argued, should be organized and allowed to participate in the formulation of a central plan, one that would result in expanded production, increased employment, a more equitable distribution, and a better balance of prices. Yet this idea, too, was thoroughly impractical when judged in terms of existing political realities. It ran counter to competitive and individualistic traditions. It threatened important vested interests. It largely ignored the complexities of the planning process or the tendency of regulated interests to dominate their regulators. And it was regarded by the majority of Americans as being overly radical, socialistic, and un-American.

Consequently, the planning of the New Deal was essentially single-industry planning, partial, piecemeal, and opportunistic, planning that could circumvent the competitive ideal or could be based on other ideals that justified making an exception. After the NRA experience, organized business groups found it increasingly difficult to devise these justifications. Some business leaders, to be sure, continued to talk about a public agency with power to waive the antitrust laws and sanction private controls.

Yet few of them were willing to accept government participation in the planning process, and few were willing to come before the public with proposals that were immediately vulnerable to charges of monopoly. It was preferable, they felt, to let the whole issue lie quiet, to rely upon unauthorized private controls, and to hope that these would be little disturbed by antitrust action. Only a few peculiarly depressed groups, like the cotton textile industry, continued to agitate for government-supported cartels, and most of these groups lacked the cohesion, power, and alternative symbols that would have been necessary to put their programs through.

In some areas, however, especially in areas where alternative symbols were present and where private controls had broken down or proven impractical, it was possible to secure a type of partial planning. Agriculture was able to avoid most of the agitation against monopoly, and while retaining to a large extent its individualistic operations, to find ways of using the state to fix prices, plan production, and regularize markets. Its ability to do so was attributable in part to the political power of the farmers, but it was also due to manipulation of certain symbols that effectively masked the monopolistic implications in the program. The ideal of the yeoman farmer—honest, independent, and morally upright—still had a strong appeal in America, and to many Americans it justified the salvation of farming as a "way of life," even at the cost of subsidies and the violation of competitive standards. Agriculture, moreover, was supposed to be the basic industry, the activity that supported all others. The country, so it was said, could not be prosperous unless its farmers were prosperous. Finally, there was the conservation argument, the great concern over conservation of the soil, which served to justify some degree of public planning and some type of production control.

Similar justifications were sometimes possible for other areas of the economy. Monopolistic arrangements in certain food-processing industries could be camouflaged as an essential part of the farm program. Departures from competitive standards in such natural resource industries as bituminous coal and crude oil production could be justified on the grounds of conservation. Public controls and economic cartelization in the fields of transportation and communication could be justified on the ground that these were "natural monopolies" in which the public had a vital interest. And in the distributive trades, it was possible to turn anti-big-business sentiment against the mass distributors, to brand them as "monopolies," and to obtain a series of essentially anti-competitive measures on the theory that they were designed to preserve competition by preserving small competitors. The small merchant, however, was never able to dodge the agitation against monopoly to the same extent that the farmer did. The supports granted him were weak to begin with, and to obtain them he had to make concessions to the competitive ideal, concessions that robbed his measures of much of their intended effectiveness.

In some ways, too, the Roosevelt Administration helped to create monopoly power for labor. Under the New Deal program, the government proceeded to absorb surplus labor and prescribe minimum labor standards; more important, it encouraged labor organization to the extent that it maintained a friendly attitude, required employer recognition of unions, and restrained certain practices that had been used to break unions in the past. For a time, the appeals to social justice, humanitarianism, and anti-big-business sentiment overrode the appeal of business spokesmen and classical economists to the competitive ideal and individualistic traditions. The doctrine that labor was not a commodity, that men who had worked and produced and kept their obligations to society were entitled to be taken care of, was widely accepted. Along with it went a growing belief that labor unions were necessary to maintain purchasing power and counterbalance big business. Consequently, even the New Dealers of an antitrust persuasion generally made a place in their program for social legislation and labor organization.

The general effect of this whole line of New Deal policy might be summed up in the word counterorganization, that is, the creation of monopoly power in areas previously unorganized. One can only conclude, however, that this did not happen according to any preconceived plan. Nor did it necessarily promote economic expansion or raise consumer purchasing power. Public support of monopolistic arrangements occurred in a piecemeal, haphazard fashion, in response to pressure from specific economic groups and as opportunities presented themselves. Since consumer organizations were weak and efforts to aid consumers made little progress, the benefits went primarily to producer groups interested in restricting production and raising prices. In the distributive trades, the efforts to help small merchants tended, insofar as they were successful, to impede technological changes, hamper mass distributors, and reduce consumer purchasing power. In the natural resource and transportation industries, most of the new legislation was designed to restrict production, reduce competition, and protect invested capital. And in the labor and agricultural fields, the strengthening of market controls was often at the expense of consumers and in conjunction with business groups. The whole tendency of interest-group planning, in fact, was toward the promotion of economic scarcity. Each group, it seemed, was trying to secure a larger piece from a pie that was steadily dwindling in size.

From an economic standpoint, then, the partial planning of the post-NRA type made little sense, and most economists, be they antitrusters, planners, or devotees of laissez-faire, felt that such an approach was doing more harm than good. It was understandable only in a political context, and as a political solution, it did possess obvious elements of strength. It retained the antitrust laws and avoided any direct attack upon the competitive ideal or competitive mythology. Yet by appealing to other goals and alternative ideals and by using these to justify special and presumably exceptional departures from competitive standards, it could make the necessary concessions to pressure groups interested in reducing competition and erecting government-sponsored cartels. Such a program might be logically inconsistent and economically harmful. Perhaps, as one critic suggested at the time, it combined the worst features of both worlds, "an impairment of the efficiency of the competitive system without the compensating benefits of rationalized collective action." But politically it was a going concern, and efforts to achieve theoretical consistency met with little success.

Perhaps the greatest defect in these limited planning measures was their tendency toward restriction, their failure to provide any incentive for expansion when an expanding economy was the crying need of the time. The easiest way to counteract this tendency, it seemed, was through government expenditures and deficit financing; in practice, this was essentially the path that the New Deal took. By 1938 Roosevelt seemed willing to accept the Keynesian arguments for a permanent spending program, and eventually, when war demands necessitated pump-priming on a gigantic scale, the spending solution worked. It overcame the restrictive tendencies in the economy, restored full employment, and brought rapid economic expansion. Drastic institutional reform, it seemed, was unnecessary. Limited, piecemeal, pressure-group planning could continue, and the spending weapon could be relied upon to stimulate expansion and maintain economic balance.

One major stream of New Deal policy, then, ran toward partial planning. Yet this stream was shaped and altered, at least in a negative sense, by its encounters with the antitrust tradition and the competitive ideal. In a time when Americans distrusted business leadership and blamed big business for the prevailing economic misery, it was only natural that an antitrust approach should have wide political appeal. Concessions had to be made to it, and these concessions meant that planning had to be limited, piecemeal, and disguised. There could be no over-all program of centralized controls. There could be no government-sponsored business commonwealth. And there could be only a minimum of government participation in the planning process.

In and of itself, however, the antitrust approach did not offer a politically workable alternative. The antitrusters might set forth their own vision of the good society. They might blame the depression upon the departure from competitive standards and suggest measures to make industrial organization correspond more closely to the competitive model. But they could never ignore or explain away the deflationary and disruptive implications of their program. Nor could they enlist much support from the important political and economic pressure groups. Consequently, the antitrust approach, like that of planning, had to be applied on a limited basis. Action could be taken only in special or exceptional areas, against unusually privileged groups that were actively hated and particularly vulnerable, in fields where one business group was fighting another, in cases where no one would get hurt, or against practices that violated common standards of decency and fairness.

This was particularly true during the period prior to 1938. The power trust, for example, was a special demon in the progressive faith, one that was actively hated by large numbers of people and one that had not only violated competitive standards but had also outraged accepted canons of honesty and tampered with democratic political ideals. For such an institution, nothing was too bad, not even a little competition; and the resulting battle, limited though its gains might be, did provide a suitable outlet for popular antitrust feeling. Much the same was also true of the other antitrust activities. Financial reform provided another outlet for antitrust sentiment, although its practical results were little more than regulation for the promotion of honesty and facilitation of the governmental spending program. The attacks upon such practices as collusive bidding, basing-point pricing, and block-booking benefited from a long history of past agitation. And the suits in the petroleum and auto-finance industries had the support of discontented business groups. The result of such activities, however, could hardly be more than marginal. When the antitrusters reached for real weapons, when they tried, for example, to use the taxing power or make drastic changes in corporate law, they found that any thorough-going program was simply not within the realm of political possibilities.

Under the circumstances, it appeared, neither planning nor antitrust action could be applied in a thorough-going fashion. Neither approach could completely eclipse the other. Yet the political climate and situation did change; and, as a result of these changes, policy vacillated between the two extremes. One period might see more emphasis on planning, the next on antitrust action, and considerable changes might also take place in the nature, content, and scope of each program.

Superficially, the crisis of 1937 was much like that of 1933. Again there were new demands for antitrust action, and again these demands were blended with new proposals for planning, rationalization, and monopolistic controls. In some respects, too, the results were similar. There was more partial planning in unorganized areas, and eventually, this was accompanied by a resumption of large-scale federal spending. The big difference was in the greater emphasis on an antitrust approach, which could be attributed primarily to the difference in political circumstances. The alienation of the business community, memories of NRA experiences, and the growing influence of antimonopolists in the Roosevelt Administration made it difficult to work out any new scheme of business-government cooperation. These same factors, coupled with the direct appeal of New Dealers to the competitive ideal, made it difficult for business groups to secure public sanction for monopolistic arrangements. The political repercussions of the recession, the fact that the new setback had occurred while the New Deal was in power, made it necessary to appeal directly to anti-big-business sentiment and to use the administered price thesis to explain why the recession had occurred and why the New Deal had failed to achieve sustained recovery. Under the circumstances, the initiative passed to the antitrusters, and larger concessions had to be made to their point of view.

One such concession was the creation of the Temporary National Economic Committee. Yet this was not so much a victory for the antitrusters as it was a way of avoiding the issue, a means of minimizing the policy conflict within the Administration and postponing any final decision. Essentially, the TNEC was a harmless device that could be used by each group to urge a specific line of action or no action at all. Antimonopolists hoped that it would generate the political sentiment necessary for a major breakthrough against concentrated economic power, but these hopes were never realized. In practice, the investigation became largely an ineffective duplicate of the frustrating debate that produced it, and by the time its report was filed, the circumstances had changed. Most of the steam had gone out of the monopoly issue, and antitrust sentiment was being replaced by war-induced patriotism.

The second major concession to antimonopoly sentiment was Thurman Arnold's revival of antitrust prosecutions, a program that presumably was designed to restore a competitive system, one in which prices were flexible and competition would provide the incentive for expansion. Actually, the underlying assumptions behind such a program were of doubtful validity. Price flexibility, even if attainable, might do more harm than good. The

Arnold approach had definite limitations, even assuming that the underlying theories were sound. It could and did break up a number of loose combinations; it could and did disrupt monopolistic arrangements that were no necessary part of modern industrialism. It could and, in some cases, did succeed in convincing businessmen that they should adopt practices that corresponded a bit more closely to the competitive model. But it made no real effort to rearrange the underlying industrial structure itself, no real attempt to dislodge vested interests, disrupt controls that were actual checks against deflation, or break up going concerns. And since the practices and policies complained of would appear in many cases to be the outgrowth of this underlying structure, the Arnold program had little success in achieving its avowed goals.

Even within these limits, moreover, Arnold's antitrust campaign ran into all sorts of difficulties. Often the combinations that he sought to break up were the very ones that the earlier New Deal had fostered. Often, even though the arrangements involved bore little relation to actual production, their sponsors claimed that they did, that their disruption would set the process of deflation in motion again and impair industrial efficiency. Arnold claimed that his activities enjoyed great popular support, and as a symbol and generality they probably did. But when they moved against specific arrangements, it was a different story. There they succeeded in alienating one political pressure group after another. Then, with the coming of war, opposition became stronger than ever. As antitrust sentiment was replaced by wartime patriotism, it seemed indeed that the disruption of private controls would reduce efficiency and impair the war effort. Consequently, the Arnold program gradually faded from the scene.

It is doubtful, then, that the innovations of 1938 should be regarded as a basic reversal in economic policy. What actually happened was not the substitution of one set of policies for another, but rather a shift in emphasis between two sets of policies that had existed side by side throughout the entire period. Policies that attacked monopoly and those that fostered it, policies that reflected the underlying dilemma of industrial America, had long been inextricably intertwined in American history, and this basic inconsistency persisted in an acute form during the nineteen thirties. Policy might and did vacillate between the two extremes; but because of the limitations of the American political structure and of American economic ideology, it was virtually impossible for one set of policies to displace the other. The New Deal reform movement was forced to adjust to this basic fact. The practical outcome was an economy characterized by private controls, partial planning, compensatory governmental spending, and occasional gestures toward the competitive ideal.

11 FROM   *James T. Patterson*
Limited by Effective Resistance

Younger than Hawley, James T. Patterson studied with two of the major figures in the postwar development of New Deal historiography and attempted to solve a problem they had debated. Born in Bridgeport, Connecticut, in 1935, Patterson was educated at Williams College and Harvard University. At Williams, he studied with James MacGregor Burns, the author of the most important one-volume biography of Roosevelt, published in 1956, and at Harvard, Patterson worked chiefly with Frank Freidel, the author of an outstanding multivolume biography of FDR, also published in the 1950's though not yet complete. While Burns criticized the President for failing to lead the nation out of the depression and to maintain the momentum of the reform movement and argued that his intellectual weaknesses were chiefly responsible for these failures, Freidel supplied a more favorable appraisal, characterized by sensitivity to political forces and the limits on the power of political leaders, and suggested, in a review, that Burns had unrealistic expectations. Burns was especially critical of Roosevelt's performance during his second term, and now Patterson looked away from the President, fo-

SOURCE. James T. Patterson, *Congressional Conservatism and the New Deal: The Growth of the Conservative Coalition in Congress, 1933–1939*, Lexington: University of Kentucky Press, 1967, pp. vii–viii, 327–337. Copyright 1967 by the publisher. Reprinted by permission of the publisher.

cused on Congress, and demonstrated that very effective opposi-
tion to the New Deal developed there in the late 1930's and that
this congressional opposition, not Roosevelt's deficiencies, limit-
ed the amount of change that Roosevelt and the New Deal could
produce. Patterson was teaching at Indiana University when his
book Congressional Conservation and the New Deal *was pub-*
lished, and it won the Frederick Jackson Turner Award of the
Organization of American Historians.

As many observers have pointed out, the formation of a conservative coalition in Congress by 1939 was one of the most significant developments of recent American political history. But
there has been no serious effort to look at the conservatives
themselves in order to answer such questions as: who were they;
what characteristics did they share; when and why did they form
a coalition; to what extent were they consciously organized; and
finally, was the coalition, such as it was, inevitable? This book
attempts to provide tentative answers to these questions.

My use of the word "conservative" may bother some readers.
Certainly no two conservatives voted alike on all major issues.
Some of these men might better be termed reactionaries, others
moderates. Many spoke the language of Social Darwinism; others were Burkean conservatives. Some were agrarian conservatives; others were spokesmen for urban business interests. But
the unifying factor, as Clinton Rossiter has pointed out, was opposition to most of the domestic program of the New Deal. By
and large the congressional conservatives by 1939 agreed in op-
posing the spread of federal power and bureaucracy, in denounc-
ing deficit spending, in criticizing industrial labor unions, and in
excoriating most welfare programs. They sought to "conserve"
an America which they believed to have existed before 1933.

[A speech in 1939 by Senator Claude Pepper of Florida] reflected one liberal interpretation of the 1939 congressional session. This view held, first of all, that Congress had hamstrung the
President, and second, that a well-organized conspiratorial coalition was responsible.

The first assumption was largely accurate. It was true that

conservatives left untouched most of the routine appropriation bills, that with the exception of Amlie and Roberts they did not interfere with presidential appointments, and that they were generous with regard to defense. They also approved reorganization bills and failed in both houses to amend either the Wagner or Fair Labor Standards acts.

But the list of administration defeats and congressional omissions was much more impressive. Roosevelt lost three successive battles over relief; he barely retrieved his devaluation powers; and he witnessed the final destruction of his undistributed-profits tax. He had to suffer the discomforts of unfriendly House investigations by Woodrum, Dies, and Smith, and he was denied so much as a shadow of his spending and housing programs. Though his requests had been modest, his success was minimal. Pepper was right about conservative success. Unquestionably, conservative congressmen had developed sufficient strength to stymie the President.

If this was a conspiracy, however, it was not so well organized as it seemed. To begin with, conservatives lacked a consistent ideology. Professing states' rights, they were willing to pass the Hatch Act, a national law regulating state primaries. Decrying deficit spending, they persisted in pouring money into farm areas, in raising the price of silver, and in toying with extravagant pension schemes. Some conservatives opposd deficit spending yet opposed raising income taxes; others were willing to lower income-tax exemptions on middle-income groups. There was a recognizable ideological difference between conservatives and liberals of the era: indeed, the 1930's revealed a split perhaps deeper than in any comparable period of American history since the 1890's. But philosophies of government were sometimes less important than the problem of which side was to grab the brass ring.

The conservative bloc also cracked along partisan lines. This problem had been obvious long before the 1939 session and would become more so as election time drew near. Conservative Democrats were already having second thoughts about defying their popular President. The percentage of Democratic opposition to the administration on major bills in 1939 was little greater in both houses than it had been in 1937–1938—despite the heady results of the 1938 elections. Partisanship, like ideological problems, prevented sustained conservative cohesion.

If these generalizations suggested the lack of conservative unity, roll-call votes proved it. Excepting the remarkable Republican solidarity, it was not easy to predict the men who would take the conservative side of any issue. On the most controversial bills in 1939 a 40- to 50-man anti-administration bloc existed in the Senate, and a more amorphous group of between 190 and 250 in the House. But the only men who consistently opposed the President were most of the Republicans and the old irreconcilable Democrats. Together, these numbered around 35 in the Senate and 180 in the House on those rare occasions when they all voted. This was certainly a more consistent core than in past congressional sessions; moreover, it would continue to operate in the future. But it was neither solid nor monolithic. As Joseph Alsop put it, "in both houses, when a pro- and anti-New Deal issue is squarely presented, a shifting population of conservative Democrats can be counted upon to join the Republicans to vote against the President. The arrangement is not formal. There is nothing calculated about it, except the Republican strategy originated by . . . McNary of refraining from arousing the Democrats' partisan feelings by inflammatory oratory."

Who were the conservatives? To begin with, they were not necessarily veterans who had outlived their era. In every session from 1933 through 1939 the percentage of veteran (pre-1933) Democrats who opposed the administration on major bills was only slightly larger than the percentage of those who rode in with the New Deal. Contrary to what might have been expected, Democratic congressmen who first served in 1933 or thereafter were not much more liberal than their predecessors. Moreover, these conservative Democrats were not all old men. Their average age in both houses was almost exactly that of their liberal colleagues.

Sectional factors were more obvious. In the Senate nearly half of the twenty-two southerners often voted against the administration on nonagricultural economic issues. Byrd, Glass, Bailey, Smith and George were among these men on most occasions, as were Harrison, Byrnes, and Connally on more than one other crucial test. In the House numbers varied, but the percentage of southerners who voted conservatively on such issues was ordinarily greater than the percentage of Democrats from other sections. This factor should not be overemphasized. Except on race legislation, the South was not "solid" in Congress. Yet on many socioeconomic issues in 1937–1939 southern Democrats were inclined to be slightly more conservative than the rest of the party.

It was also true that most congressional conservatives rose from middle or upper middle class stock, that they were well educated, and that they reflected the views of conservative farmers and businessmen in their districts. Burke, for instance, often echoed the antilabor position of the National Association of Manufacturers, and in 1942 he would become president of a coal producers association. Glass was friendly with several Wall Street bankers, and George was frank to admit his partiality for private power interests in Georgia. Others, such as Tydings and Gerry, cherished friendships with prominent conservative businessmen in their home states. Many rural conservatives had few contacts with large corporate interests but more often than not were friendly with small-town bankers, businessmen, and manufacturers. Howard Smith was one of these, and Taber, Cox, and Snell three others. These congressmen possessed little feeling of identification with organized labor, Negroes, tenant farmers, or other deprived groups pressing for social welfare.

Those few conservatives whose youth had been poor or who had once belonged to the ranks of organized labor had long since cast off such influences and had adopted an ethic of rugged individualism typical of many self-made men. Martin, for instance, recalled his youthful adversities fondly, congratulating himself upon his diligence and thrift. Donahey of Ohio, a one-time journeyman printer, believed equally staunchly in self-help and frugality. So did Gore, Vandenberg, and others whose backgrounds might otherwise have conditioned them to look more favorably on the desires of the underprivileged. These congressmen tended to share the views of conservative businessmen, especially on relief spending, labor bills, and tax policy.

Perhaps the most distinguishing characteristic of the congressional conservative of the period was the nature of his district. Those who represented predominantly urban districts usually sided with the administration on economic and social issues, whereas those from heavily rural districts often defied the administration after 1936. Rural southerners, for instance, were more consistently conservative than urban southerners. And eastern urban Democrats were usually the most dependable. In this sense it should not be surprising that there was a conservative upsurge after 1936, for it was then that the heavily northern-urban character of the New Deal became most obvious, and most ominous, to conservatives.

If these characteristics distinguished the congressional conservatives, what was responsible for increased conservative success after 1936? Part of the reason was the shrewdness and power of a few strategically placed individuals: McNary's overall strategy, Martin's organization in the House, Garner's pervasive influence in both houses. Another reason was the normal lack of leverage belonging to administrations completing their second terms. Personal animosities certainly contributed; the Democrats whom Roosevelt tried to purge delighted in evening the score. Many moderates, seeking a breathing spell in 1935, merely awaited an occasion to proclaim their independence. Finally, Roosevelt's continued aggressiveness made him few friends. Far from conceding ground to advance his foreign policy, as has sometimes been asserted, he persisted in his feeling that "the people are with me." Roosevelt by no means "caused" the conservative coalition, but with measures such as the court plan he hastened its development, and with actions such as the purge he helped to steel its resolve.

Nothing so simple as a "conspiracy" or "failure of presidential leadership" accounted for the conservative renaissance. The main reasons were at once partisan, psychological, institutional, issue-based, and constituent-based. The biggest difference between the 1939 session and its predecessors was, after all, the presence in 1939 of so many Republicans. In the Senate they formed, for the first time since 1934, at least half the conservative bloc. In the more rebellious House Republicans formed some three-fourths of anti-administration strength on every close issue. The administration was in trouble from the first day of the session.

A change in congressional psychology was perhaps more significant. The events of 1937–1938 not only gave renewed confidence to conservative congressmen, but they intensified long-submerged feelings of congressional independence, particularly in the House, which was more responsive to the most recent election. In this sense the period from 1933 to 1936 was a Great Aberration: it was the only peacetime period in twentieth-century American history when a Chief Executive was so generally successful in dominating his Congress. Thus, although the sessions of 1937–1939 witnessed the emergence of a new kind of conservative bloc, they were also more simply a return to the normality of presidential-congressional hostility. Had external events given congressmen confidence earlier, they probably would have kicked over the traces before 1937. That they did when presidential prestige declined should occasion no surprise.

The institutional nature of Congress reinforced this return to normality. The system of congressional representation in the 1930's was distinctly favorable to the rural areas of America, many of which were one-party areas as well. This situation was most obvious in the Senate, where southern, Plains, and Rocky Mountain senators filled half the chamber. Inequitable representation also existed in the House. Before 1937 the nationwide emergency had obscured rural-urban divisions by forcing even rural conservatives to support emergency legislation. But after 1937 few rural areas faced a crisis comparable to that of 1933–1935. Most rural congressmen remained anxious to support special-interest legislation beneficial to their districts but not to assist measures for the relief of urban problems. To rural members such measures deprived their districts of funds which they might otherwise have received themselves. Urban congressmen, clamoring loudly after 1937 for help, too often found the simple problem of rural overrepresentation too great an obstacle.

The nature of the major congressional issues after 1936 was especially conducive to this kind of urban-rural division. Whether there were two New Deals prior to 1936 is a debatable point. In retrospect, however, it seems that a different kind of New Deal developed after 1936. From the largely southern-western party of 1933 the Democratic party had become a coalition in which northern urban elements dominated. Issues dear to these northern urbanites—relief spending, housing, prolabor bills—accordingly formed major points of congressional controversy, whether Roosevelt desired them or not. Thus it was not surprising that Roosevelt faced greater opposition from the rural members of both Houses. Most of these rural congressmen had acceded to measures such as social security and even the Wagner Act in 1935. But when urban Democrats demanded more aid after 1936, they balked. It was this "new" and unplanned New Deal, the frankly urban liberalism of men such as Wagner, that many formerly reliable rural congressmen determined to oppose after 1936.

The rise of congressional conservatism also reflected changing constituent attitudes. In many ways the state of America's economic health in 1939 was little better than it had been in 1934, and it might have been expected that economic impulses behind reform would have increased—or at least have remained steady. Yet after 1936 conservative congressmen were able to defy the New Deal without fear of reprisal from their constituents. Why was it that hard-pressed voters did not demand stronger measures after 1936?

The answer, it seems in retrospect, was complex. Many constituents did continue to demand federal action to relieve their problems, but their demands were parochial and essentially selfish. Beset with their own economic needs, they were often apathetic otherwise. Farmers excitedly demanded more money for agriculture; union leaders insisted upon legislation beneficial to organized labor; city machines requested higher relief and public works expenditures; and spokesmen for slum dwellers demanded a cluster of bills to relieve urban misery. These varied groups were able to unite successfully in presidential elections. They were even strong enough to influence congressional voting— farm bills and pump-priming were cases in point. But they never formed a unified working coalition in Congress, and because their orientation was distinctly local instead of national they failed to reach a consensus on many broad social welfare programs. To liberals it is a distressing thought, but the voting behavior of nonconservatives in Congress from 1937 through 1939 exhibited little more breadth of vision—and a good deal less unity of purpose—than the behavior of conservatives. The conservative coalition was less than monolithic, but liberals, more disparate as a group and faced with the more difficult problem of agreeing upon a positive program, were hardly a coalition at all.

Moreover, the economic situation of 1933–1934 was considerably different from that in 1937 or in 1938–1939. As early as 1937 many moderates believed that the emergency was over and that the New Deal should adhere to the breathing spell promised them in 1935. The relationship between economic conditions and periods of social reform remains a debatable historical point, but in 1937 improved times helped to diminish the ardor of many congressmen for relief and reform.

The recession which followed also differed considerably from the depression period of 1933–1934. Though economic hardship persisted, attitudes changed. In 1933 most business and community leaders were discredited, and congressmen, reacting to the strongest pressures, responded to the administration, not to the silent and confused power groups in their constituencies. But in 1935 many businessmen began to turn against the New Deal, and by 1937, no longer afraid of chaos, they freely castigated it. These conservative community leaders never recovered the status that they had enjoyed in 1929, but they did reassert their voices in public policy. Many moderate congressmen, dissatisfied with the New Deal for a variety of reasons—patronage, bureaucracy, spending—listened more carefully to such influential men than they had in 1933–1935. This renewed constituent determination helped account for the opposition of urban as well as rural congressmen to such measures as the undistributed-profits tax.

Congressmen had also become impatient by 1938. By then the New Deal was no longer new, and to many it had had ample time to prove itself as an agent of recovery. Its failure to end the Depression and its inability to avoid a recession damned it in conservative eyes. More important—and less obvious—the recession convinced many nonconservatives of the administration's economic naiveté. To these congressmen it appeared that an administration that could not solve the economic problem was also unqualified to speak authoritatively on such measures as regional development, executive reorganization, taxes, or labor policy. This lack of certainty among nonconservatives facilitated the conservative task after 1936.

Political factors also contributed to the strength of congressional conservatism. For all his power and prestige, the President was unable to dominate state political parties, and nominations of Democrats on the state level continued to be matters for state bosses to determine. Because even the disastrous Depression was slow to destroy American attitudes toward such matters as balanced budgets, federal power, and labor unions, state and local machines, reflecting this attitudinal inertia, continued to nominate and elect congressmen whose views were either moderate or business-oriented. Or they nominated men whose liberalism extended only to tapping the Treasury for purely local gains. The result was the election of many congressmen whose sense of loyalty to the New Deal was limited and who depended for reelection upon the powerful groups in their constituencies. Against this kind of situation presidential resources were of limited value.

12 FROM   *Barton J. Bernstein*
The Continuation of Corporate Capitalism

A contemporary of Patterson's and also a student of Freidel's, Barton J. Bernstein was much more critical of the New Dealers and the New Deal. Born in New York City in 1936 and educated at Queens College, Washington University, and Harvard University, he now teaches at Stanford and is a major contributor to the literature on the Truman administration. The book from which the following selection was taken was designed to make New Left interpretations of American history available to the public. New Left scholars were profoundly dissatisfied with American historiography in the postwar period; they were convinced that its dominant assumptions had been shattered by the major events of the 1960's, and Bernstein challenged the histori-

SOURCE. Barton J. Bernstein, "The New Deal: The Conservative Achievements of Liberal Reform," in Bernstein, ed., *Towards a New Past: Dissenting Essays in American History,* New York: Pantheon Books, 1968, pp. 264–265, 267–272, 273–278, 280–282. Copyright © 1968 by Random House, Inc. Reprinted by permission of the publisher.

ans of the New Deal who had written "from a liberal democratic consensus" and "praised the Roosevelt administration for its nonideological flexibility and for its far-ranging reforms."

The liberal reforms of the New Deal did not transform the American system; they conserved and protected American corporate capitalism, occasionally by absorbing parts of threatening programs. There was no significant redistribution of power in American society, only limited recognition of other organized groups, seldom of unorganized peoples. Neither the bolder programs advanced by New Dealers nor the final legislation greatly extended the beneficence of government beyond the middle classes or drew upon the wealth of the few for the needs of the many. Designed to maintain the American system, liberal activity was directed toward essentially conservative goals. Experimentalism was most frequently limited to means; seldom did it extend to ends. Never questioning private enterprise, it operated within safe channels, for short of Marxism or even of native American radicalisms that offered structural critiques and structural solutions.

All of this is not to deny the changes wrought by the New Deal—the extension of welfare programs, the growth of federal power, the strengthening of the executive, even the narrowing of property rights. But it is to assert that the elements of continuity are stronger, that the magnitude of change has been exaggerated. The New Deal failed to solve the problem of depression, it failed to raise the impoverished, it failed to redistribute income, it failed to extend equality and generally countenanced racial discrimination and segregation. It failed generally to make business more responsible to the social welfare or to threaten business's pre-eminent political power. In this sense, the New Deal, despite the shifts in tone and spirit from the earlier decade, was profoundly conservative and continuous with the 1920s.

Using the federal government to stabilize the economy and advance the interests of the groups, Franklin D. Roosevelt directed the campaign to save large-scale corporate capitalism. Though recognizing new political interests and extending benefits to them, his New Deal never effectively challenged big business or the organization of the economy. In providing assistance to the needy and by rescuing them from starvation, Roosevelt's humane efforts also protected the established system: he sapped organized radicalism of its waning strength and of its potential consistuency among the unorganized and discontented. Sensitive to public opinion and fearful of radicalism, Roosevelt acted from a mixture of motives that rendered his liberalism cautious and limited, his experimentalism narrow. Despite the flurry of activity, his government was more vigorous and flexible about means than goals, and the goals were more conservative than historians usually acknowledge.

Roosevelt's response to the banking crisis emphasizes the conservatism of his administration and its self-conscious avoidance of more radical means that might have transformed American capitalism. Entering the White House when banks were failing and Americans had lost faith in the financial system, the President could have nationalized it—"without a word of protest," judged Senator Bronson Cutting. "If ever there was a moment when things hung in the balance," later wrote Raymond Moley, a member of the original "brain trust," "it was on March 5, 1933—when unorthodoxy would have drained the last remaining strength of the capitalistic system." To save the system, Roosevelt relied upon collaboration between bankers and Hoover's Treasury officials to prepare legislation extending federal assistance to banking. So great was the demand for action that House members, voting even without copies, passed it unanimously, and the Senate, despite objections by a few Progressives, approved it the same evening. "The President," remarked a cynical congressman, "drove the money-changers out of the Capitol on March 4th—and they were all back on the 9th."

Undoubtedly the most dramatic example of Roosevelt's early conservative approach to recovery was the National Recovery Administration (NRA). It was based on the War Industries Board (WIB) which had provided the model for the campaign of Bernard Baruch, General Hugh Johnson, and other former WIB officials during the twenties to limit competition through industrial self-regulation under federal sanction. As trade associations flourished during the decade, the FTC encouraged "codes of fair competition" and some industries even tried to set prices and restrict production. Operating without the force of law, these agreements broke down. When the depression struck, industrial pleas for regulation increased. After the Great Crash, important business leaders including Henry I. Harriman of the Chamber of Commerce and Gerard Swope of General Electric called for suspension of antitrust laws and federal organization of business collaboration. Joining them were labor leaders, particularly those in "sick" industries—John L. Lewis of the United Mine Workers and Sidney Hillman of Amalgamated Clothing Workers.

Designed largely for industrial recovery, the NRA legislation provided for minimum wages and maximum hours. It also made concessions to pro-labor congressmen and labor leaders who demanded some specific benefits for unions—recognition of the worker's right to organization and to collective bargaining. In practice, though, the much-heralded Section 7a was a disappointment to most friends of labor. (For the shrewd Lewis, however, it became a mandate to organize: "The President wants you to join a union.") To many frustrated workers and their disgusted leaders, NRA became "National Run Around." The clause, unionists found (in the words of Brookings economists), "had the practical effect of placing NRA on the side of anti-union employers in their struggle against trade unions. . . . [It] thus threw its weight against labor in the balance of bargaining power." And while some far-sighted industrialists feared radicalism and hoped to forestall it by incorporating unions into the economic system, most preferred to leave their workers unorganized or in company unions. To many businessmen, large and independent unions as such seemed a radical threat to the system of business control.

Not only did the NRA provide fewer advantages than unionists had anticipated, but it also failed as a recovery measure. It probably even retarded recovery by supporting restrictionism and price increases, concluded a Brookings study. Placing effective power for code-writing in big business, NRA injured small businesses and contributed to the concentration of American industry. It was not the government-business partnership as envisaged by Adolf A. Berle, Jr., nor government managed as Rexford Tugwell had hoped, but rather, business managed, as

Raymond Moley had desired. Calling NRA "industrial self-government," its director, General Hugh Johnson, had explained that
"NRA is exactly what industry organized in trade associations
makes it." Despite the annoyance of some big businessmen with
Section 7a, the NRA reaffirmed and consolidated their power at
a time when the public was critical of industrialists and finan-
ciers.

Viewing the economy as a "concert of organized interests,"
the New Deal also provided benefits for farmers—the Agricultural Adjustment Act. Reflecting the political power of larger
commercial farmers and accepting restrictionist economics, the
measure assumed that the agricultural problem was overproduction, not underconsumption. Financed by a processing tax designed to raise prices to parity, payments encouraged restricted
production and cutbacks in farm labor. With benefits accruing
chiefly to the larger owners, they frequently removed from production the lands of sharecroppers and tenant farmers, and
"tractored" them and hired hands off the land. In assisting agriculture, the AAA, like the NRA, sacrificed the interests of the
marginal and the unrecognized to the welfare of those with greater political and economic power.

In large measure, the early New Deal of the NRA and AAA
was a "broker state." Though the government served as a media-
tor of interests and sometimes imposed its will in divisive situations, it was generally the servant of powerful groups. "Like the
mercantilists, the New Dealers protected vested interests with the
authority of the state," acknowledges William Leuchtenburg. But
it was some improvement over the 1920s when business was the
only interest capable of imposing its will on the government.
While extending to other groups the benefits of the state, the
New Deal, however, continued to recognize the pre-eminence of
business interests.

The politics of the broker state also heralded the way of the
future—of continued corporate dominance in a political structure where other groups agreed generally on corporate capitalism
and squabbled only about the size of the shares. Delighted by
this increased participation and the absorption of dissident
groups, many liberals did not understand the dangers in the
emerging organization of politics. They had too much faith in

representative institutions and in associations to foresee the perils —of leaders not representing their constituents, of bureaucracy diffusing responsibility, of officials serving their own interests. Failing to perceive the dangers in the emerging structure, most liberals agreed with Senator Robert Wagner of New York: "In order that the strong may not take advantage of the weak, every group must be equally strong." His advice then seemed appropriate for organizing labor, but it neglected the problems of unrepresentative leadership and of the many millions to be left beyond organization.

In dealing with the organized interests, the President acted frequently as a broker, but his government did not simply express the vectors of external forces. The New Deal state was too complex, too loose, and some of Roosevelt's subordinates were following their own inclinations and pushing the government in directions of their own design. The President would also depart from his role as a broker and act to secure programs he desired. As a skilled politician, he could split coalitions, divert the interests of groups, or place the prestige of his office on the side of desired legislation.

In seeking to protect the stock market, for example, Roosevelt endorsed the Securities and Exchange measure (of 1934), despite the opposition of many in the New York financial community. His advisers split the opposition. Rallying to support the administration were the out-of-town exchanges, representatives of the large commission houses, including James Forrestal of Dillon, Read, and Robert Lovett of Brown Brothers, Harriman, and such commission brokers as E. A. Pierce and Paul Shields. Opposed to the Wall Street "old guard" and their companies, this group included those who wished to avoid more radical legislation, as well as others who had wanted earlier to place trading practices under federal legislation which they could influence.

Though the law restored confidence in the securities market and protected capitalism, it alarmed some businessmen and contributed to the false belief that the New Deal was threatening business. But it was not the disaffection of a portion of the business community, nor the creation of the Liberty League, that menaced the broker state. Rather it was the threat of the Left— expressed, for example, in such overwrought statements as Min-

nesota Governor Floyd Olson's: "I am not a liberal . . . I am a
radical. . . . I am not satisfied with hanging a laurel wreath on
burglars and thieves . . . and calling them code authorities or
something else." While Olson, along with some others who succumbed to the rhetoric of militancy, would back down and sof-
ten their meaning, their words dramatized real grievances: the
failure of the early New Deal to end misery, to re-create prosperity. The New Deal excluded too many. Its programs were inade-
quate.

While Roosevelt reluctantly endorsed relief and went beyond
Hoover in support of public works, he too preferred self-liqui-
dating projects, desired a balanced budget, and resisted spending
the huge sums required to lift the nation out of depression.

For millions suffering in a nation wracked by poverty, the
promises of the Left seemed attractive. Capitalizing on the misery, Huey Long offered Americans a "Share Our Wealth" program—a welfare state with prosperity, not subsistence, for the
disadvantaged, those neglected by most politicians. "Every Man
a King": pensions for the elderly, college for the deserving,
homes and cars for families—that was the promise of American
life. Also proposing minimum wages, increased public works,
shorter work weeks, and a generous farm program, he demanded
a "soak-the-rich" tax program. Despite the economic defects of
his plan, Long was no hayseed, and his forays into the East revealed support far beyond the bayous and hamlets of his native
South. In California discontent was so great that Upton Sinclair,
food faddist and former socialist, captured the Democratic nomination for governor on a platform of "production-for-use"—factories and farms for the unemployed. "In a cooperative society,"
promised Sinclair, "every man, woman, and child would have
the equivalent of $5,000 a year income from labor of the able-
bodied young men for three or four hours per day." More chal-
lenging to Roosevelt was Francis Townsend's plan—monthly
payments of $200 to those past sixty who retired and promised
to spend the stipend within thirty days. Another enemy of the
New Deal was Father Coughlin, the popular radio priest, who
had broken with Roosevelt and formed a National Union for Social Justice to lead the way to a corporate society beyond capitalism.

To a troubled nation offered "redemption" by the Left, there was also painful evidence that the social fabric was tearing—law was breaking down. When the truckers in Minneapolis struck, the police provoked an incident and shot sixty-seven people, some in the back. Covering the tragedy, Eric Sevareid, then a young reporter, wrote, "I understood deep in my bones and blood what fascism was." In San Francisco union leaders embittered by police brutality led a general strike and aroused national fears of class warfare. Elsewhere, in textile mills from Rhode Island to Georgia, in cities like Des Moines and Toledo, New York and Philadelphia, there were brutality and violence, sometimes bayonets and tear gas.

Challenged by the Left, and with the new Congress more liberal and more willing to spend, Roosevelt turned to disarm the discontent. "Boys—this is our hour," confided Harry Hopkins. "We've got to get everything we want—a works program, social security, wages and hours, everything—now or never. Get your minds to work on developing a complete ticket to provide security for all the folks of this country up and down and across the board." Hopkins and the associates he addressed were not radicals: they did not seek to transform the system, only to make it more humane. They, too, wished to preserve large-scale corporate capitalism, but unlike Roosevelt or Moley, they were prepared for more vigorous action. Their commitment to reform was greater, their tolerance for injustice far less. Joining them in pushing the New Deal left were the leaders of industrial unions, who, while also not wishing to transform the system, sought for workingmen higher wages, better conditions, stronger and larger unions, and for themselves a place closer to the fulcrum of power.

The problems of organized labor, however, neither aroused Roosevelt's humanitarianism nor suggested possibilities of reshaping the political coalition. When asked during the NRA about employee representation, he had replied that workers could select anyone they wished—the Ahkoond of Swat, a union, even the Royal Geographical Society. As a paternalist, viewing himself (in the words of James MacGregor Burns) as a "partisan and benefactor" of workers, he would not understand the objections to company unions or to multiple unionism under NRA.

Nor did he foresee the political dividends that support of independent unions could yield to his party. Though presiding over the reshaping of politics (which would extend the channels of power to some of the discontented and redirect their efforts to competition within a limited framework), he was not its architect, and he was unable clearly to see or understand the unfolding design.

When Senator Wagner submitted his labor relations bill, he received no assitance from the President and even struggled to prevent Roosevelt from joining the opposition. The President "never lifted a finger," recalls Miss Perkins. ("I, myself, had very little sympathy with the bill," she wrote.) But after the measure easily passed the Senate and seemed likely to win the House's endorsement, Roosevelt reversed himself. Three days before the Supreme Court invalidated the NRA, including the legal support for unionization, Roosevelt came out for the bill. Placing it on his "must" list, he may have hoped to influence the final provisions and turn an administration defeat into victory.

Responding to the threat from the left, Roosevelt also moved during the Second Hundred Days to secure laws regulating banking, raising taxes, dissolving utility-holding companies, and creating social security. Building on the efforts of states during the Progressive Era, the Social Security Act marked the movement toward the welfare state, but the core of the measure, the old-age provision, was more important as a landmark than for its substance. While establishing a federal-state system of unemployment compensation, the government, by making workers contribute to their old-age insurance, denied its financial responsibility for the elderly. The act excluded more than a fifth of the labor force leaving, among others, more than five million farm laborers and domestics without coverage.

Though Roosevelt criticized the tax laws for not preventing "an unjust concentration of wealth and economic power," his own tax measure would not have significantly redistributed wealth. Yet his message provoked an "amen" from Huey Long and protests from businessmen. Retreating from his promises, Roosevelt failed to support the bill, and it succumbed to conservative forces. They removed the inheritance tax and greatly reduced the proposed corporate and individual levies. The final law did not "soak the rich." But it did engender deep resentment among the wealthy for increasing taxes on gifts and estates, imposing an excess-profits tax (which Roosevelt had not requested), and raising surtaxes. When combined with such regressive levies as social security and local taxes, however, the Wealth Tax of 1935 did not drain wealth from higher-income groups, and the top one percent even increased their shares during the New Deal years.

Those historians who have characterized the events of 1935 as the beginning of a second New Deal have imposed a pattern on those years which most participants did not then discern. In moving to social security, guarantees of collective bargaining, utility regulation, and progressive taxation, the government did advance the nation toward greater liberalism, but the shift was exaggerated and most of the measures accomplished far less than either friends or foes suggested. Certainly, despite a mild bill authorizing destruction of utilities-holding companies, there was no effort to atomize business, no real threat to concentration.

Nor were so many powerful businessmen disaffected by the New Deal. Though the smaller businessmen who filled the ranks of the Chamber of Commerce resented the federal bureaucracy and the benefits to labor and thus criticized NRA, representatives of big business found the agency useful and opposed a return to unrestricted competition. In 1935, members of the Business Advisory Council—including Henry Harriman, outgoing president of the Chamber, Thomas Watson of International Business Machines, Walter Gifford of American Telephone and Telegraph, Gerard Swope of General Electric, Winthrop Aldrich of the Chase National Bank, and W. Averell Harriman of Union Pacific—vigorously endorsed a two-year renewal of NRA.

When the Supreme Court in 1935 declared the "hot" oil clause and then NRA unconstitutional, the administration moved to measures known as the "little NRA." Reestablishing regulations in bituminous coal and oil, the New Deal also checked wholesale price discrimination and legalized "fair trade" practices. Though Roosevelt never acted to revive the NRA, he periodically contemplated its restoration. In the so-called second

New Deal, as in the "first," government remained largely the benefactor of big business, and some more advanced businessmen realized this.

Roosevelt could attack the "economic royalists" and endorse the TNEC investigation of economic concentration, but he was unprepared to resist the basic demands of big business. While there was ambiguity in his treatment of oligopoly, it was more the confusion of means than of ends, for his tactics were never likely to impair concentration. Even the antitrust program under Thurman Arnold, concludes Frank Freidel, was "intended less to bust the trusts than to forestall too drastic legislation." Operating through consent degrees and designed to reduce prices to the consumer, the program frequently "allowed industries to function much as they had in NRA days." In effect, then, throughout its variations, the New Deal had sought to cooperate with business.

Though vigorous in rhetoric and experimental in tone, the New Deal was narrow in its goals and wary of bold economic reform. Roosevelt's sense of what was politically desirable was frequently more restricted than others' views of what was possible and necessary. Roosevelt's limits were those of ideology; they were not inherent in experimentalism. For while the President explored the narrow center, and some New Dealers considered bolder possibilities, John Dewey, the philosopher of experimentalism, moved far beyond the New Deal and sought to reshape the system. Liberalism, he warned, "must now become radical. . . . For the gulf between what the actual situation makes possible and the actual state itself is so great that it cannot be bridged by piecemeal policies undertaken *ad hoc*." The boundaries of New Deal experimentalism, as Howard Zinn has emphasized, could extend far beyond Roosevelt's cautious ventures. Operating within very safe channels, Roosevelt not only avoided Marxism and the socialization of property, but he also stopped far short of other possibilities—communal direction of production or the organized distribution of surplus. The President and many of his associates were doctrinaires of the center, and their maneuvers in social reform were limited to cautious excursions.

Usually opportunistic and frequently shifting, the New Deal was restricted by its ideology. It ran out of fuel not because of the conservative opposition, but because it ran out of ideas. Acknowledging the end in 1939, Roosevelt proclaimed, "We have now passed the period of internal conflict in the launching of our program of social reform. Our full energies may now be released to invigorate the processes of recovery in order to preserve our reforms. . . ."

The sad truth was that the heralded reforms were severely limited, that inequality continued, that efforts at recovery had failed. Millions had come to accept the depression as a way of life. A decade after the Great Crash, when millions were still unemployed, Fiorello LaGuardia recommended that "we accept the inevitable, that we are now in a new normal." "It was reasonable to expect a probable minimum of 4,000,000 to 5,000,000 unemployed," Harry Hopkins had concluded. Even that level was never reached, for business would not spend and Roosevelt refused to countenance the necessary expenditures. "It was in economics that our troubles lay," Tugwell wrote. "For their solution his [Roosevelt's] progressivism, his new deal was pathetically insufficient. . . .

Clinging to faith in fiscal orthodoxy even when engaged in deficit spending, Roosevelt had been unwilling to greatly unbalance the budget. Having pledged in his first campaign to cut expenditures and to restore the balanced budget, the President had at first adopted recovery programs that would not drain government finances. Despite a burst of activity under the Civil Works Administration during the first winter, public works expenditures were frequently slow and cautious. Shifting from direct relief, which Roosevelt (like Hoover) considered "a narcotic, a subtle destroyer of the human spirit," the government moved to work relief. ("It saves his skill. It gives him a chance to do something socially useful," said Hopkins.") By 1937 the government had poured enough money into the economy to spur production to within 10 percent of 1929 levels, but unemployment still hovered over seven million. Yet so eager was the President to balance the budget that he cut expenditures for public works and relief, and plunged the economy into a greater depression. While renewing expenditures, Roosevelt remained cautious in his fiscal policy, and the nation still had almost nine million unemployed in 1939. After nearly six years of struggling with the depression, the

Roosevelt administration could not lead the nation to recovery, but it had relieved suffering. In most of America, starvation was no longer possible. Perhaps that was the most humane achievement of the New Deal.

Its efforts on behalf of humane *reform* were generally faltering and shallow, of more value to the middle classes, of less value to organized workers, of even less to the marginal men. In conception and in practice, seemingly humane efforts revealed the shortcomings of American liberalism. For example, public housing, praised as evidence of the federal government's concern for the poor, was limited in scope (to 180,000 units) and unfortunate in results. It usually meant the consolidation of ghettos, the robbing of men of their dignity, the treatment of men as wards with few rights. And slum clearance came to mean "Negro clearance" and removal of the other poor. Of much of this liberal reformers were unaware, and some of the problems can be traced to the structure of bureaucracy and to the selection of government personnel and social workers who disliked the poor. But the liberal conceptions, it can be argued, were also flawed for there was no willingness to consult the poor, nor to encourage their participation. Liberalism was elitist. Seeking to build America in their own image, liberals wanted to create an environment which they thought would restructure character and personality more appropriate to white, middle-class America.

It was not in the cities and not among the Negroes but in rural America that Roosevelt administration made its (philosophically) boldest efforts: creation of the Tennessee Valley Authority and the later attempt to construct seven little valley authorities. Though conservation was not a new federal policy and government-owned utilities were sanctioned by municipal experience, federal activity in this area constituted a challenge to corporate enterprise and an expression of concern about the poor. A valuable example of regional planning and a contribution to regional prosperity, TVA still fell far short of expectations. The agency soon retreated from social planning. ("From 1936 on," wrote Tugwell, "the TVA should have been called the Tennessee Valley Power Production and Flood Control Corporation.") Fearful of antagonizing the powerful interests, its agricultural program neglected the tenants and the sharecroppers.

To urban workingmen the New Deal offered some, but limited, material benefits. Though the government had instituted contributory social security and unemployment insurance, its much-heralded Fair Labor Standards Act, while prohibiting child labor, was a greater disappointment. It exempted millions from its wages-and-hours provisions. So unsatisfactory was the measure that one congressman cynically suggested, "Within 90 days after appointment of the administrator, she should report to Congress whether anyone is subject to this bill." Requiring a minimum of twenty-five cents an hour ($11 a week for 44 hours), it raised the wages of only about a half-million at a time when nearly twelve million workers in interstate commerce were earning less than forty cents an hour.

More important than these limited measures was the administration's support, albeit belated, of the organization of labor and the fight of collective bargaining. Slightly increasing organized workers' share of the national income, the new industrial unions extended job security to millions who were previously subject to the whim of management. Unionization freed them from the perils of a free market.

By assisting labor, as well as agriculture, the New Deal started the institutionalization of larger interest groups into a new political economy. Joining business as tentative junior partners, they shared the consensus on the value of large-scale corporate capitalism, and were permitted to participate in the competition for the division of shares. While failing to redistribute income, the New Deal modified the political structure at the price of excluding many from the process of decision making. To many what was offered in fact was symbolic representation, formal representation. It was not the industrial workers necessarily who were recognized, but their unions and leaders; it was not even the farmers, but their organizations and leaders. While this was not a conscious design, it was the predictable result of conscious policies. It could not have been easily avoided, for it was part of the price paid by a large society unwilling to consider radical new designs for the distribution of power and wealth.

In the deepest sense, this new form of representation was rooted in the liberal's failure to endorse a meaningful egalitarianism which would provide actual equality of opportunity. It was also the limited concern with equality and justice that accounted for the shallow efforts of the New Deal and left so many Americans behind. The New Deal was neither a "third American Revolution," as Carl Degler suggests, nor even a "half-way revolution," as William Leuchtenburg concludes. Not only was the extension of representation to new groups less than full-fledged partnership, but the New Deal neglected many Americans—sharecroppers, tenant farmers, migratory workers and farm laborers, slum dwellers, unskilled workers, and the unemployed Negroes. They were left outside the new order. As Roosevelt asserted in 1937 (in a classic understatement), one third of the nation was "ill-nourished, ill-clad, ill-housed."

Yet, by the power of rhetoric and through the appeals of political organization, the Roosevelt government managed to win or retain the allegiance of these peoples. Perhaps this is one of the crueller ironies of liberal politics, that the marginal men trapped in hopelessness were seduced by rhetoric, by the style and movement, by the symbolism of efforts seldom reaching beyond words. In acting to protect the institution of private property and in advancing the interests of corporate capitalism, the New Deal assisted the middle and upper sectors of society. It protected them, sometimes, even at the cost of injuring the lower sectors. Seldom did it bestow much of substance upon the lower classes. Never did the New Deal seek to organize these groups into independent political forces. Seldom did it risk antagonizing established interests. For some this would constitute a puzzling defect of liberalism; for some, the failure to achieve true liberalism. To others it would emphasize the inherent shortcomings of American liberal democracy. As the nation prepared for war, liberalism, by accepting private property and federal assistance to corporate capitalism, was not prepared effectively to reduce inequities, to redistribute political power, or to extend equality from promise to reality.

13 FROM   *Jerold S. Auerbach*
          Radical Change Far Short of Revolution

Not all of the New Deal historians who came of age in the late 1950's discarded the generally positive appraisal of the New Deal that had dominated historical writing on it when they had reached the graduate schools. Jerold S. Auerbach was born in Philadelphia in the same year in which Bernstein was born in New York City (1936) and was a graduate student at Columbia University while Bernstein studied at Harvard. Also like Bernstein, Auerbach studied with one of the leading historians of the New Deal in the postwar period. Auerbach's mentor was William E. Leuchtenburg, author of the widely acclaimed survey Franklin D. Roosevelt and the New Deal *(1963). In it, Leuchtenburg recognized shortcomings but emphasized accomplishments and called the New Deal a revolution—or at least a "halfway revolution." As the following essay indicates, Auerbach, then a historian at Brandeis University and now at Wellesley College, was closer to Leuchtenburg than to Bernstein in his estimate of the New Deal's significance. The author of* Labor and Liberty: The La Follette Committee and the New Deal *(1966), Auerbach regarded the legal protection that the New Deal gave to the industrial worker as one of its most significant and valuable accomplishments.*

In a time of rampant social criticism, when American verities seem precarious, the past no less than the present falls under scrutiny. Indeed, past and present lose their very separateness. Present issues guide research into the past; historians call upon

SOURCE. Jerold S. Auerbach, "New Deal, Old Deal, or Raw Deal: Some Thoughts on New Left Historiography," *Journal of Southern History*, xxxv (February 1969), pp. 18–30. Copyright 1969 by the Southern Historical Association. Reprinted by permission of the Managing Editor.

the past to speak to present needs; strident demands are heard for a "new" or "usable" past. Just as turn-of-the-century progressive ferment provided the setting for Charles A. Beard's reinterpretation of the Founding Fathers and the Depression elicited Matthew Josephson's discovery of the "robber barons," so current social issues promise to leave new eddies of historical revisionism in their wake. Revisionist historians, like automobile drivers, learn to keep one eye on the rearview mirror while the other scans the road ahead.

Given the focus of current protest—against racism, imperialism, liberalism, the power elite, bureaucratic centralization, and the very nature of corporate capitalism—it is understandable that the New Deal should become a prime target for revisionist fire. In a dual sense the particular achievements and failures of the Roosevelt administration become both compelling and galling. First, because it is so alluring to consider March 1933 as *tabula rasa,* after which New Dealers quickly dissipated the last best hope for a drastic restructuring of American society. And second, because presumably we are now reaping the noxious harvest of welfare capitalism whose seeds the New Dealers sowed three decades ago. As historian Irwin Unger has observed, "the New Deal is the immediate source of the liberal welfare state, and they [New Left critics] despise it as much as they do the flaccid, self-satisfied society that they hold is its direct descendant." Thus one critic complains: "Most of the time America is an ugly place to live in. All the 'reforms' only seem to have made it uglier. And more sophisticated in its evil. . . . In the long run, what *did* the New Deal do? Besides the Smith Act?" Another laments the reluctance of historians to discuss "in what way and to what extent the New Deal . . . contributed to the rise of the political, economic, and social conditions we are familiar with today." According to a third, the New Deal "launched the American welfare state, a brand new, large, ungainly infant, destined to survive all the hazards of childhood and a maladjusted adolescence, eventually to mature in the Great Society . . . ."

The bill of grievances compiled by New Left critics against the New Deal makes the Roosevelt administration seem more ominous even than the reign of George III, which prompted an ear-

lier declaration of independence. Manifold causes impel the critics to their separation from previously favorable estimates of the
New Deal. These include the absence of any philosophy of reform; the consequent failure of New Dealers even to attack,
much less resolve, fundamental social problems; a commitment
to the salvation of corporate capitalism; destruction of the Left;
remoteness from popular authority and indifference to participatory democracy. Running through this jeremiad is the refrain
made explicit by Paul Conkin: "The story of the New Deal is a
sad story, the ever recurring story of what might have been."

Conkin, more than any of the critics with whom he is here associated, concedes that the New Deal initiated "some important
modifications of the American economic system." Considering
what might have been, however, its record was spotty and disappointing: ". . . no core of political principles, no clear economic
philosophy, no new clarification of the dilemmas of liberal democracy" emerged from the New Deal. Without them, apparently, little else matters. Conkin is especially eager to smite the can-
ard that the New Deal was pragmatic, or even experimental.
"Above all," he writes, "Roosevelt was not a pragmatist." And
experimentalism, Conkin adds, means "the advocacy, in terms of
what is known, of a tentative solution, as comprehensive, as systematic, as consistent, as formally perfect as possible, and then
as careful a testing of the tentative answer as circumstances permit . . . ." The New Deal, Conkin complains, "denied the idea
of experimentation—clear hypotheses and controlled verifica-
tion."

The flaw in this model—as Conkin himself concedes—is that
in politics circumstances do not very often permit careful tests of
tentative answers. Because political leaders are not scientists, because people are not chemicals, and because life is not a test
tube, laboratory metaphors are deceptive. Scientists are not necessarily compelled to dilute their experiments in order to complete them, nor must they submit their results to a national elec-
torate for approval. In tearing the mantle of pragmatism from
the shoulders of New Dealers, Conkin and others have only
demonstrated the incompatibility of pragmatism, defined as a
formal system of thought, with politics. By their definition, *no*
political administration can be pragmatic; the term is without

meaning in a political context. Instead of waving the "bloody shirt" of pragmatism, therefore, both defenders and critics of the New Deal would do well to pass beyond pragmatic shadows to substance.

Far more serious is the allegation that the New Deal failed to resolve, or even to attack, fundamental social problems. It is around this proposition that a cluster of New Left critics of the New Deal have directed their most concentrated assault. Lloyd C. Gardner asks: "How many of the society's fundamental problems had really been corrected, or even attacked? How real had the recovery been? How dangerous the path taken?" Howard Zinn suggests that the New Deal failed to solve the most fundamental problem confronting it: "how to bring the blessings of immense natural wealth and staggering productive potential to every person in the land." Barton J. Bernstein complains that "The New Deal failed to solve the problem of depression, it failed to raise the impoverished, it failed to redistribute income, it failed to extend equality and generally countenanced racial discrimination and segregation."

The premise upon which these criticisms rest is the impossibility of solutions to "fundamental problems" short of "a radically new economic equilibrium" and a "significant redistribution of power in American society. . . ." Yet this is a slippery premise at best, with several concealed semantic traps. By definition, "fundamental" problems become those which the New Deal did not solve. A "radically new economic equilibrium" seems tantamount to any equilibrium that the New Deal failed to attain. And "significant redistribution of power" means any redistribution beyond the one actually achieved. Of course, if total repudiation of capitalism becomes the sole test by which to measure the New Deal, obviously it (like every preceding and subsequent administration) failed. But critics who apply this test should at least begin to indicate its relevance within the context of a political system whose voters and leaders have persistently refused to sanction the destruction of capitalism as a goal.

If any point short of total repudiation is acceptable, then the issue may be fairly joined. New Left critics concede a new legal framework for labor-management relations; new controls over banks, stock exchanges, and other institutions of private enterprise; social security; relief; public housing and public works; the restoration of jobs to at least half the jobless; legitimization of a new economic role for government; and a profound political and constitutional shake-up. Yet, according to Bernstein for example, "seemingly humane [reform] efforts" by New Dealers only "revealed the shortcomings of American liberalism." One is compelled to inquire: Did they seem humane because they *were* humane, in which case Bernstein's point is lost; or did they seem humane despite the fact that they were *not* humane, in which case we desperately need a new definition of "humane." Furthermore, against what standard of the thirties are liberalism's "shortcomings" measured? How fruitful is it to label New Deal efforts at slum clearance and public housing (or other reforms) as "faltering and shallow," when the point of reference for this judgment clearly is 1968, not 1938?

The subject of race relations, a pressing current concern but for many and legitimate reasons *not* a paramount New Deal issue, understandably attracts attention from New Left critics. Black Americans, Bernstein concedes, did receive (minimal) aid and (cautious) recognition. But Roosevelt should not be too quickly praised, for even if the results were commendable, bad reasons negate them. Rather than making color the basis of assistance, the New Deal dispensed aid on the basis of need. This distinction seemed less important to Negroes than to Bernstein, who uneasily balances his judgment that "the New Deal left intact the race relations of America" with the fact that it was able "to woo Negro leaders and even to court the masses." According to Conkin Negro support for the New Deal arose from that fact that Negroes were "politically purchased by relief or by the occasional concern of bureaucrats. . . ." Unless one assumes, as Bernstein, Conkin, and others elsewere assume, that the New Deal was so diabolically clever that it won the support of those whom it did *not* help, one must conclude that most black (and white) Americans found much in the New Deal to command their allegiance.

In addition to social welfare and race, labor relations can serve as a useful litmus test of the New Deal record. Surprisingly, New Left critics have little to say about the single most vital issue for Old Leftists. In manifold ways, the resolution of capital-labor discord represented the most enduring and compelling need in American public life. This vexing problem, with its serious economic, political, and constitutional ramifications, had lingered since the nation's earliest years as an industrial power. Without legal protection for the right to organize and bargain collectively, industrial workers were helpless in the face of concerted employer power. It was precisely this legal protection that the New Deal provided, albeit with reluctance in presidential circles.

The New Left critics demur, insisting *Plus ça change, plus c'est la même chose*. Bernstein concedes change but insists that its significance was merely "the institutionalization of larger interest groups into a new political economy. . . . It was not the industrial workers necessarily who were recognized, but their unions and leaders. . . ." Brad Wiley, noting the forces of industrial unionism unleashed by New Deal laws, complains that the CIO merely "furthered the process of rationalization of the economy by disciplining the working class through containing the militancy of the workers, eliminating the threat of strikes, and generally mediating between the boss and 'his' workers." This line of argument, of course, creates a neat whipsaw effect. Whether the New Deal ignored labor or succored it, New Deal culpability is assured. Criticized for only slowly awakening to workers' grievances and aspirations, the New Deal is criticized equally strenuously for eradicating the major sources of their discontent.

Bernstein and Wiley carry their portable whipsaw one step further. Each feels compelled to note New Deal reforms, but neither will accept mere reform as sufficient. In fact, reform becomes destructive—more destructive, paradoxically, than failure to reform. According to Bernstein: "The liberal reforms of the New Deal did not transform the American system; they conserved and protected American corporate capitalism, *occasionally by absorbing parts of threatening programs*." Wiley maintains: "The New Deal's *recognition of potentially antagonistic social groups* served a conservative integrating purpose. If these groups could be led to cooperate with the dominant economic and political elite on the basis of the rules of corporate capitalism, any possibility that their demands for reform might begin to question fundamental property relations was eliminated."

What especially seems to perturb the New Left critics is the very willingness of the New Deal to absorb radical proposals into its own program. This might be interpreted to reveal both the viability of many radical demands and New Deal responsiveness to pressure from the Left. New Left critics have, however, taken a different sounding. Conkin observes sadly that Roosevelt's 1936 landslide "almost destroyed the political left in American politics, whether dogmatic fringe groups or the terribly honest and flexible American Socialist Party." Bernstein seems to regret New Deal assistance to the needy, because "Roosevelt's humane efforts also protected the established system: he sapped organized radicalism of its waning strength and of its potential constituency among the unorganized and discontented." Zinn notes the emergence of a plethora of protest groups and complains that "there was no political program around which these disparate groups could effectively unite. And many of them began to lose their thrust *when their demands were partially met.*"

Implicit in this critique is an assumption that the New Deal undercut radical reform. This assumption is highly questionable; at the very least it requires more documentation and less assertion. It is more than conceivable that a depression without the New Deal would have produced no reform at all. Such was the American experience between 1930 and 1932. The New Deal may well have made radical reform, to the extent that it existed, possible. We know that radicalism flourished more in the wake of New Deal reforms of 1933 and 1935 than in anticipation of them. A sense of possibilities, elicited by the Roosevelt administration, repeatedly galvanized the Left. Tocqueville's insight that endured evils become intolerable when avenues of escape are opened is especially relevant in this context. This certainly was true in labor-management relations: radicals launched their most successful forays from the legal fortifications erected under the National Industrial Recovery Act and the National Labor Relations Act, Radicals, like factory workers and sharecroppers, waged a revolution of rising expectations. The success (unintended, of course) of the New Deal in stimulating and even legitimizing radical ferment would seem to warrant more attention from New Left critics than it has received.

Instead, in a pamphlet entitled *Historians and the New Deal*, published by the Madison Students for a Democratic Society,

Brad Wiley plays the most dissonant variation on this theme. Wiley, who distinguishes between economic recovery and social reform, properly maintains that "the stabilization of the capitalist system as a political objective is in no way a necessary precondition for effective social reform." The New Deal, he concedes, may have represented "a new *form* of government intervention in the economy," but the results were predictable: "the role of the state continues to subordinate the problems of reform and reorganization of urban-industrial society to those of recovery and stabilization in the corporate-capitalist system of production." Whether emphasis is placed on recovery or reform, the New Deal record was dismal. Incredibly, however, Wiley cites its very failure to generate recovery as "symptomatic of the fact that the 1930s were not as severe a social crisis as historians have characterized it." The basis for this sweeping *non sequitur* is Wiley's observation that "no major social group or class . . . felt themselves sufficiently threatened to commit themselves to more extreme forms of political and economic action." Reasoning from his conclusions back to the evidence, Wiley extrapolates from the absence of "extreme forms of . . . action" the absence of any severe crisis at all after 1929. The Depression seemingly is but a figment of the historical imagination, contrived to delude the gullible into believing that massive unemployment, starvation, and suffering had some social significance. Since the objective situation, according to Wiley, was only a mirage, the entire welfare-state apparatus of the New Deal, instead of representing a real response to a real need, served merely as "an ideological tool in the baggage of modern capitalism."

From the perspective of the 1960's, which for New Left critics provides the only relevant standard, one of the most serious of New Deal deficiencies was its alleged remoteness from sources of popular authority—four presidential and numerous congressional victories to the contrary notwithstanding. A curious ambivalence pervades New Left analysis of this issue. Wiley, for example, argues that New Deal centralizing tendencies served "to isolate government further from popular authority. . . ." Concentration of power in executive agencies meant that policies were formulated and implemented "by Presidential advisers and . . . technicians none of whom are ever directly answerable to the commonwealth they ostensibly serve." Zinn moves one step further to claim that "Only the aggrieved themselves can provide the motive power to create that new deal which neither FDR nor JFK nor LBJ gave us." Yet Zinn himself asserts that "the boldest programs" and "the largest expectations" came not from the aggrieved, but "from intellectuals not closely associated with the White House, from those whose ideological reach is not impaired by their clinking glasses with the mighty." New Deal half measures, Conkin concurs, were repudiated by "the more alienated, more sensitive, and more analytic intellectuals," who were "too honest and too clear-headed" to "master the soothing art of the fireside . . . ."

Again, the categories are so neat and functional: the New Deal allegedly shunned participatory democracy, yet the most innovative alternatives came not from the demos but from a powerless intellectual elite. *Ipso facto,* intellectuals who held power were corrupted by it; intellectuals without power could only wallow in their own sensitivity and alienation. Conveniently, so long as they remained remote from power their ideas retained force and energy. But the moment they arrived in Washington to apply these forceful ideas energetically they were guilty of a sell-out. So loud was the noise of "clinking glasses" that serious intellectual discourse was obliterated. By definition, intellectual contributions could be made only by those who opted for purity over power.

Imprisoned by their assumption that the New Deal offered so little to so many, New Left critics find themselves hard-pressed to explain why the Roosevelt administration received such enthusiastic popular mandates. Bernstein proposes that "the marginal men trapped in hopelessness were seduced by rhetoric. . . ." Conkin conjectures that downtrodden Negroes were "politically purchased." Again the whipsaw: Had marginal men *not* voted for Roosevelt, it would prove New Deal programmatic deficiencies. That they *did* vote for him indicates only the power of rhetoric—or relief. (It is revealing that Bernstein's application of the notion of rhetorical seduction does not extend to radicals like Huey Long or Father Coughlin, whose slogans, "Every Man a King" and "Social Justice," certainly were far more seductive—in the dictionary meaning of leading someone astray—than Roosevelt's program.) Since opposition to the New Deal is the only posture consistent with New Left interpretations of New Deal defects, support of the New Deal, in a somewhat patronizing fashion, becomes a measure of the folly of those who failed to appreciate where their true interests lay. Indeed, Conkin even argues that opponents "misconstrued the direction of the New Deal. . . . The enemies of the New Deal were wrong. They should have been friends." Rather than assume, as the evidence warrants, that enemies and friends of the New Deal realistically pursued legitimate conceptions of their own self-interest, New Left critics transform ardent admirers into "real" enemies and vigorous critics into misguided friends.

Perplexity mounts when one recalls Conkin's assertion regarding the New Deal as "a sad story . . . of what might have been." This refrain resounds throughout Conkin's essay: Roosevelt "might have" acted differently during the 1932–1933 interregnum; the administration "might have" encouraged recovery and "might have" restored confidence in 1933. "*If* Roosevelt had not, by 1936, turned in devastating fury upon business. . . . *If* Roosevelt . . . had really turned toward increased federal direction and ownership. Of *if* the government . . . had pumped such enormous sums of borrowed money into the economy that it had to respond." But one sour note mars the crescendo. In his penultimate paragraph Conkin asserts: "The plausible alternatives to the New Deal are not easily suggested, particularly if one considers all the confining and limiting circumstances." The hypothesizing, then, was for naught; the critic has become tacit defender, leaving the New Deal imprisoned by circumstance and thereby implicitly exonerated for its deficiencies.

It should by now be apparent that the New Left critique of the New Deal—spirited, controversial, and provocative though it may be—is occasionally illogical and consistently ahistorical. This dour estimate is in no way intended as a blessing for all that the New Deal did or failed to do—or for all that its defenders have said or left unsaid about it. Nor, most emphatically, does it imply that all criticism of the New Deal is unwelcome, for the uniformly favorable treatment of the New Deal which has prevailed for two decades is indeed in need of revision. Rather, it is an assertion that the New Left critique is sterile because New

Left critics have applied irrelevant standards and a protean vocabulary to reach a priori conclusions. It is hardly necessary for them to display surprise (or indignation) at their "discovery" that the New Deal saved capitalism and refused to abandon private property. No one has seriously doubted this; indeed, the New Deal received no mandate to do otherwise. Its Old Left critics were numerically overwhelmed by those who wanted little more than the reshuffling of an old deck. Its New Left critics are trying to win a verdict in the history books that was decisively rejected thirty years ago. Lloyd C. Gardner, referring to Roosevelt's defenders, has observed: "Any incongruities which turned up in the legend of the New Deal were carefully tucked away in chapters called 'Behind the Mask,' where human errors and failings all became part of the 'enigma' that was Franklin Roosevelt." Yet it is equally true that Roosevelt's detractors have applied to the New Deal ex post facto standards of judgment that would render every administration since Washington's equally culpable. It is, in fact, the search for culpability rather than the quest for understanding that looms as the most prominent—and characteristic—defect of the New Left critique.

Howard Zinn, for example, would have historians "consider present needs at the expense, if necessary, of old attachments." If these were the sole alternatives, Zinn's position would have more to recommend it. But they are not. The historian who is a partisan for or against the present deprives himself of the insights that only come after he permits the present to frame his questions and insists that the past alone provide his answers—on *its* terms, not his. If it is understandable that the interest of historians in the abolitionists should be rekindled in an era of intensive civil rights activity, it would nonetheless be a betrayal of the historian's function to berate ante-bellum egalitarians for pursuing *their* goals and tactics rather than those of the freedom riders and black nationalists of the 1960's. Similarly, while generations of New Deal historians predictably will be guided by the questions and methodology of *their* present, their evaluations of the New Deal will remain suspect so long as they judge New Dealers harshly (or indeed kindly) for misbehaving in the thirties according to the gospel of the New Left in the sixties. Historians blessed with twenty-twenty hindsight who flail their forebears for

lacking twenty-twenty foresight are themselves plagued by my-
opia. If men in public life today are imprisoned by New Deal
categories and solutions, it is they who are the proper targets of
criticism, not those who innovated so successfully thirty-five
years ago that their program set the terms of political discourse
not only for their generation but for succeeding ones.

To speak of innovation is not, of course, to speak of revolution. At the very least, New Left critics have demonstrated the
futility of debating—as historians did until fairly recently—
whether the New Deal was evolutionary or revolutionary. Yet if
it is now apparent that those who endured the Depression (especially those who suffered least) tended from the perspective of
their own past to magnify change, it is equally apparent that
New Left critics have jumped to the opposite extreme. Not only
have they occasionally played with words in an effort to transform liberal reform into conservatism; in the process they have
also slighted those changes which, measured by this country's
past (although not by our present), substantially reallocated
power in American society. In so doing they have refused to
grapple with the difficult analytical problem of the nature of revolutionary, or even radical, change.

Recent theoretical literature suggests that revolution consti-
tutes one stage along a continuum of social change. "Revolutionary" change denotes nothing less than a change of the established political order by violence; according to one student of the
process it is *an illegal change of the conditions of legality.*" Under this definition nonviolent revolution would be a contradiction
in terms. "Rebellion" is a less extreme form of social change, in
which the essential ingredient is an illegal change of persons in
authority rather than of the system itself. Clearly, the New Deal
constituted neither a revolution nor a rebellion. But, as political
scientist Chalmers Johnson suggests, basic change can occur
without resort to violence; he cites the New Deal as one example
of radical, albeit nonrevolutionary, change. Johnson conjectures
that the United States may well have avoided a revolution during
the Depression because Roosevelt inaugurated "a drastic program of reform to restore confidence in the system. . . ." Given
the Depression as a form of severe disequilibrium, the New Deal
becomes comprehensible as radical change to restore an old

equilibrium. "Creative political action," Johnson writes, "is the specific antidote to revolutionary conditions. . . ." But New Deal efforts to restore the old equilibrium could not always be contained; its creative action impelled political and social currents to overflow old channels. By 1937 the result was radical change far short of revolution. Precisely this fact, needless to say, enrages New Left critics.

William E. Leuchtenburg has written that "the changes wrought in the 1930's—the growth in power of the national government, the advance toward a Welfare State, the unionizing of industrial America, the subsidization of the farmer, the Supreme Court 'revolution,' the upheaval in political alignments—make the decade one of the most significant periods in American history." Unless one is prepared to defend the proposition that by definition any change short of revolution is meaningless change, this is indeed an impressive record, one which few administrations before or since can match. To concede this is hardly to imply that all was done that could, or should, have been done. Contemporary critics, even within the administration, knew otherwise. Rexford G. Tugwell recently has written: "At some moments I thought Roosevelt saw how radical a reconstruction was called for; at others I guessed that he would temporize. . . . I was right in this last. The New Deal was a mild medicine." Roosevelt, Tugwell complains, "could have emerged from the orthodox progressive chrysalis and led us into a new world. He chose rather rickety repairs for an old one."

New Left critics would agree: Americans lived by the tenets of corporate capitalism before Roosevelt came into office; by shoring up discredited capitalist institutions the New Deal perpetuated a corrupt, destructive system which brought the nation logically and inevitably to the brink of international and national cataclysm—in the streets of Saigon and in the streets of American cities. Such absolute moral judgments can neither be proved nor disproved; hence their appeal. Furthermore, they are quite irrelevant to historical analysis if history is to remain distinct from propaganda for or against current policies. This is not to insist, however, that the New Deal (or any era) be measured only against its past. Although the configurations of the future were not, and could not have been, even dimly perceptible in the

1930's, historians retain the freedom, denied to contemporaries, to measure an era against both its subsequent and its antecedent developments. But historians who concentrate exclusively on either, as the New Left critics have done, take an implicit vow to write one-dimensional history. They repudiate the subtle interaction of the historical past and the historian's present for the sharp thrust of current political protest. Historians of the *post*-New Deal era, along with Paul Conkin, may properly maintain that "The United States has neither moved beyond it [the New Deal] nor searched for valid alternatives." This fact will disappoint New Left critics, and others, but it is incumbent upon them to recognize that the onus of responsibility devolves upon those who have governed since 1941, not upon the New Dealers. Even historiographical victories cannot be won against the wrong enemy in the wrong place at the wrong time.

Suggestions for Further Reading

Some of the most important surveys of the New Deal have already been mentioned. See especially the large work by Arthur Schlesinger, Jr., *The Age of Roosevelt* (3 vols., New York, 1957–1960); and the shorter study by Leuchtenburg, *Franklin D. Roosevelt and the New Deal* (New York, 1963). Also valuable are Basil Rauch, *The History of the New Deal* (New York, 1944, 1963); Dixon Wecter, *The Age of the Great Depression 1929–1941* (New York, 1948); and Dennis Brogan, *The Era of Franklin Roosevelt* (New Haven, 1950). On the debate that Rauch opened up over the ways in which the New Deal developed, see Otis L. Graham, Jr., "Historians and the New Deals, 1944–1960," *Social Studies*, 54 (1963), 133–140; and William H. Wilson, "The Two New Deals: A Valid Concept?" *Historian*, 28 (1966), 268–288. On the performance of the economic system during the 1930's see Robert Aaron Gordon, *Business Fluctuations* (New York, 1961); John Chamberlain, *The Enterprising Americans: A Business History of the United States* (New York, 1963); and Douglas C. North, *Growth and Welfare in the American Past: A New Economic History* (Englewood Cliffs, 1966).

There are several very valuable books on Franklin Roosevelt. The most impressive and thorough account of his pre-presidential years is found in the three-volume work by Frank Freidel,

Franklin D. Roosevelt (Boston, 1952–1956) . James MacGregor Burns published a provocative and very important volume on Roosevelt before World War II, *Roosevelt: The Lion and the Fox* (New York, 1956) , and recently added a volume on the war years, *Roosevelt: The Soldier of Freedom* (New York, 1970) . Also valuable are Bernard Bellush, *Franklin D. Roosevelt as Governor of New York* (New York, 1955) ; Daniel R. Fusfeld, *The Economic Thought of Franklin D. Roosevelt and the Origins of the New Deal* (New York, 1956) ; Thomas H. Greer, *What Roosevelt Thought: The Social and Political Ideas of Franklin D. Roosevelt* (East Lansing, 1958) ; Morton J. Frisch, "Roosevelt the Conservator: A Rejoinder to Hofstadter," *Journal of Politics,* 25 (1963) , 361–372; and Alfred B. Rollins, Jr., *Roosevelt and Howe* (New York, 1962) . Richard A. Watson, Jr., "Franklin D. Roosevelt in Historical Writing, 1950–1957," *South Atlantic Quarterly,* 57 (1958) , 104–126; and Clarke A. Chambers, "FDR: Pragmatist-Idealist," *Pacific Northwest Quarterly,* 52 (1961) , 50–55, are useful surveys of the early Roosevelt literature; and Leuchtenburg, ed., *Franklin D. Roosevelt: A Profile* (New York, 1967) , supplies a rich sample of the literature. On one of the controversial sides of FDR's career see Richard S. Kirkendall, "Franklin D. Roosevelt and the Service Intellectual," *Mississippi Valley Historical Review,* 49 (1962) , 456–471.

Other New Dealers are examined in John Morton Blum, *From the Morgenthau Diaries* (3 vols., Boston, 1959–1967) ; Bernard Sternsher, *Rexford Guy Tugwell and the New Deal* (New Brunswick, 1964) ; Searle F. Charles, *Minister of Relief: Harry Hopkins and the Depression* (Syracuse, 1963) ; and Edward L. and Frederick H. Schapsmeier, *Henry A. Wallace of Iowa: The Agrarian Years, 1910–1940* (Ames, 1968) .

On the importance of Roosevelt's Public Papers see Samuel B. Hand, "Rosenman, Thucydides, and the New Deal," *Journal of American History,* 55 (1968) , 334–348. On the value of the Roosevelt Library see Richard S. Kirkendall, "Presidential Libraries—One Researcher's Point of View," *The American Archivist,* 25 (1962) , 441–448; H. G. Jones, *The Records of a Nation: Their Management, Preservation and Use* (New York, 1969) ; and *Final Report of the Joint AHA-OAH Ad Hoc Com-*

mittee to Investigate the Charges Against the Franklin D. Roosevelt Library and Related Matters (Washington, D.C., and Bloomington, 1970). And on the rapid appearance and the value of the New Deal memoirs see David M. Potter, "Sketches for the Roosevelt Portrait," *The Yale Review,* 39 (1949), 39–53; and Frank Freidel, "Are There Too Many New Deal Diaries?" *American Heritage,* 6 (1955), 109–112. Among the most important memoirs are Raymond Moley, *After Seven Years* (New York, 1939), and *The First New Deal* (New York, 1966); and Rexford Guy Tugwell, *The Democratic Roosevelt: A Biography of Franklin D. Roosevelt* (Garden City, 1957), and *The Brains Trust* (New York, 1968).

New Deal business policies have been examined by several scholars in addition to Ellis Hawley. Especially important are Sidney Fine, *The Automobile Industry Under the Blue Eagle: Labor, Management, and the Automobile Manufacturing Code* (Ann Arbor, 1963); Louis Galombos, *Competition & Cooperation: The Emergence of a National Trade Association* (Baltimore, 1966); Ralph F. De Bedts, *The New Deal's S E C: The Formative Years* (New York, 1964); Cedric B. Cowing, *Populists, Plungers, and Progressives: A Social History of Stock and Commodity Speculation* (Princeton, 1965); Gerald D. Nash, *United States Oil Policy, 1890–1964: Business and Government in Twentieth Century America* (Pittsburgh, 1968); Michael E. Parrish, *Securities Regulation and the New Deal* (New Haven, 1970); Charles O. Johnson, *Food and Drug Legislation in the New Deal* (Princeton, 1970); and Susan Estabrook Kennedy, *The Banking Crisis* (Lexington, 1973). On fiscal policies see also Robert Lekachman, *The Age of Keynes* (New York, 1966); and Herbert Stein, *The Fiscal Revolution* in America (Chicago, 1969).

Students interested in The New Deal should also consult historians of business and the businessman. See, for example, Thomas C. Cochran, *The American Business System: A Historical Perspective, 1900–1955* (Cambridge, 1957); Forrest McDonald, *Let There be Light: The Electric Utility Industry in Wisconsin, 1881–1955* (Madison, 1957); Raymond C. Miller, *Kilowatts at Work: A History of the Detroit Edison Co.,* (Detroit, 1957); J. Carlyle Buley, *The American Life Convention,*

1906–1952: A Study in the History of Life Insurance (New York, 1953) ; Henrietta Larson and Kenneth Wiggins Porter, *History of Humble Oil and Refining Company: A Study in Industrial Growth* (New York, 1959) ; Boris Emmett and John E. Jeuck, *Catalogues and Counters: A History of Sears, Roebuck and Company* (Chicago, 1950) ; Loren Baritz, *The Servants of Power: A History of the Use of Social Science in American Industry* (Middletown, 1960) ; Otis Pease, *The Responsibilities of American Advertising: Private Control and Public Influence, 1920–1940* (New Haven, 1958) ; Allan Nevins and Frank Ernest Hill, *Ford: Decline and Rebirth, 1933–1962* (New York, 1963) ; Vincent P. Carosso, *Investment Banking in America: A History* (Cambridge, 1970) ; and Morrell Heald, *The Social Responsibilities of Business: Company and Community, 1900–1960* (Cleveland, 1970) .

New Deal agricultural politics and policies have attracted a substantial amount of attention from historians. For a broad survey see Murray R. Benedict, *Farm Policies of the United States, 1790–1950: A study of Their Origins and Development, 1790–1950* (New York, 1953) . The following, while focusing on specific groups, hit many parts of the story: Christiana M. Campbell, *The Farm Bureau and the New Deal: A Study of the Making of a National Farm Policy, 1933–1940* (Urbana, 1962) ; and Richard S. Kirkendall, *Social Scientists and Farm Politics in the Age of Roosevelt* (Columbia, 1966) . Van L. Perkins, *Crisis in Agriculture: The Agricultural Adjustment Administration and the New Deal, 1933* (Berkeley and Los Angeles, 1969) , examines the major developments in a crucial period. John Shover explores the significant failure of one protest movement in *Cornbelt Rebellion: The Farmers' Holiday Association* (Urbana, 1965) . David E. Conrad, *The Forgotten Farmers: The Story of the Sharecroppers and the New Deal* (Urbana, 1965) ; Sidney Baldwin, *Poverty and Politics: The Rise and Decline of the Farm Security Administration* (Chapel Hill, 1968) ; Louis Cantor, *A Prologue to the Protest Movement: The Missouri Sharecropper Roadside Demonstration of 1939* (Durham, 1969) ; Raymond Wolters, *Negroes and the Great Depression: The Problem of Economic Recovery* (Westport, 1970) ; and Donald H. Grubbs, *Cry from the Cotton: The Southern Tenant*

Farmers' Union and the New Deal (Chapel Hill, 1971), are concerned with the New Deal's relations with the rural poor. See also Paul K. Conkin, *Tomorrow a New World: The New Deal Community Program* (Ithaca, 1959); and Leonard J. Arrington, "Western Agriculture and the New Deal," *Agricultural History,* 44 (1970), 337–354. These authors develop a significant debate over the importance and value of the New Deal farm programs.

Irving Bernstein's *Turbulent Years: A History of the American Worker 1933–1941* (Boston, 1969) is the best survey of the New Deal and labor while Jerold Auerbach's *Labor and Liberty: The La Follette Committee and the New Deal* (Indianapolis, 1966) is a more specialized but very valuable study. Also very important on the subject are Milton Derber and Edwin Young, eds., *Labor and the New Deal* (Madison, 1957); James O. Morris, *Conflict Within the AFL: A Study of Craft Versus Industrial Unionism, 1901–1938* (Ithaca, 1958); Philip Taft, *The A. F. of L. from the Death of Gompers to the Merger* (New York, 1959); Walter Galenson, *The CIO Challenge to the AFL: A History of the American Labor Movement, 1935–1941* (Cambridge, 1960); David Brody, *The Butcher Workmen: A Study of Unionization* (Cambridge, 1964); Richard C. Cortner, *The Wagner Act Cases* (Knoxville, 1964); and Sidney Fine, *Sit-Down: The General Motors Strike of 1936–1937* (Ann Arbor, 1969). Fine's earlier work on the NRA should also be seen.

On relief and social welfare, in addition to Chambers and Charles, consult Robert H. Bremner, *From the Depths: The Discovery of Poverty in America* (New York, 1956); Timothy L. McDonnell, S. J., *The Wagner Housing Act: A Case Study of the Legislative Process* (Chicago, 1957); Abraham Holtzman, *The Townsend Movement: A political Study* (New York, 1963); John A. Salmond, *The Civilian Conservation Corps, 1933–1942: A New Deal Case Study* (Durham, 1967); Jane DeHart Mathews, *The Federal Theater, 1935–1939: Plays, Relief, and Politics* (Princeton, 1967); Theron F. Schlabach, *Edwin E. Witte: Cautious Reformer* (Madison, 1969); Daniel Nelson, *Unemployment Insurance: The American Experience, 1915–1935* (Madison, 1969); and Daniel S. Hirshfield, *The Lost Reform: The Campaign for Compulsory Health Insurance in the United States from 1932 to 1943* (Cambridge, 1970).

These studies present a picture of a rather slow evolution of the welfare state.

The failure of the left is also important for students of the New Deal. See especially Bernard Sternsher's outstanding effort to solve the problem of the left's failure in his introduction to *Hitting Home: The Great Depression in Town and Country* (Chicago, 1970). On the Socialist party, compare David A. Shannon, *The Socialist Party of America: A History* (New York, 1955), and Murray B. Seidler, *Norman Thomas: Respectable Rebel* (Syracuse, 1961), with Bernard K. Johnpoll, *Pacifist's Progress: Norman Thomas and the Decline of American Socialism* (Chicago, 1970). Irving Howe and Lewis Coser, *The American Communist Party: A Critical History, 1919–1957* (Boston, 1957); and Frank A. Warren III, *Liberals and Communism: The "Red Decade" Revisited* (Bloomington, 1966), are important works on communism and the Communist party. On other varieties of leftism see Edward C. Blackorby, *Prairie Rebel: The Public Life of William Lemke* (Lincoln, 1963); Charles J. Tull, *Father Coughlin and the New Deal* (Syracuse, 1965); David H. Bennett, *Demagogues in the Depression: American Radicals and the Union Party, 1932–1936* (New Brunswick, 1969), and T. Harry Williams, *Huey Long* (New York, 1969).

On crucial working-class support for Roosevelt and the New Deal, see, in addition to the books already cited by Bernstein and Derber and Young, Irving Bernstein, *The Lean Years: A History of the American Worker 1920–1933* (Boston, 1960); Samuel Lubell, *The Future of American Politics* (Garden City, 1952); Walter Johnson, *1600 Pennsylvania Avenue: Presidents and the People, 1929–1959* (Boston, 1960); Carl N. Degler, "American Political Parties and the Rise of the City: An Interpretation," *Journal of American History*, 51 (1964), 41–59; J. Joseph Huthmacher, *Massachusetts People and Politics 1919–1933* (Cambridge, 1959); Franklin D. Mitchell, *Embattled Democracy: Missouri Democratic Politics, 1919–1932* (Columbia, 1968); and John M. Allswang, *A Home for All Peoples: Ethnic Politics in Chicago, 1890–1936* (Lexington, 1971).

On resistance to change, George Wolfskill, *The Revolt of the Conservatives: A History of the American Liberty League, 1934–1940* (Boston, 1962); and Morton Keller, *In Defense of*

Yesterday: James M. Beck and the Politics of Conservatism, 1861–1936 (New York, 1958), are especially important works on the unsuccessful Liberty League. On the growing conservatism in Congress see, in addition to Patterson, Richard Polenberg, *Reorganizing Roosevelt's Government: The Controversy over Executive Reorganization, 1936–1939* (Cambridge, 1966); and John Robert Moore, *Senator Josiah Bailey of North Carolina: A Political Biography* (Durham, 1968). Dewey W. Grantham, Jr., *The Democratic South* (Athens, 1963); Frank Freidel, *F.D.R. and the South* (Baton Rouge, 1965); and George Brown Tindall, *The Emergence of the New South, 1913–1945* (Baton Rouge, 1967), are of major importance on the South and the New Deal. On the situation within the Democratic party in the late 1930's, see Bernard F. Donahoe, *Private Plans and Public Dangers: The Story of FDR's Third Nomination* (Notre Dame, 1965). On the Republican party in the 1930's see George H. Mayer, *The Republican Party 1854–1964;* (New York, 1964); Donald R. McCoy, *Landon of Kansas* (Lincoln, 1966); and Donald Bruce Johnson, *The Republican Party and Wendell Willkie* (Urbana, 1960). Patterson has also written a book that emphasizes the strength of resistance to change at the state and local levels, *The New Deal and the States: Federalism in Transition* (Princeton, 1969).

While many of the works mentioned pay some attention to intellectual developments in the 1930's, these developments have received more attention recently. See Paul A. Carter, *The Decline and Revival of the Social Gospel: Social and Political Liberalism in American Protestant Churches, 1920–1940* (Ithaca, 1956); Robert Moats Miller, *American Protestantism and Social Issues, 1919–1939* (Chapel Hill, 1958); Donald B. Meyer, *The Protestant Search for Political Realism, 1919–1941* (Berkeley and Los Angeles, 1960); David J. O'Brien, *American Catholics and Social Reform: The New Deal Years* (New York, 1968); Charles C. Alexander, *Nationalism in American Thought, 1930–1945:* (Chicago, 1969); and Arthur Ekirch, *Ideologies and Utopias: The Impact of the New Deal on American Thought* (Chicago, 1969).

Several historians, in addition to Schlesinger and Commager, have stressed the New Deal's links with the Progressive movement. See especially, Eric Goldman, *Rendezvous with Destiny: A History of Modern American Reform* (New York, 1953); Arthur Link, *American Epoch: A History of the United States Since the 1890's* (New York, 1955); and Andrew M. Scott, "The Progressive Era in Perspective," *Journal of Politics,* 21 (1959), 685–701. See also Solomon Fabricant, *The Trend of Government Activity in the United States Since 1900* (New York, 1952); and Richard S. Kirkendall, "The Great Depression: Another Watershed in American History?" in John Braeman et al., eds., *Change and Continuity in Twentieth Century America* (Columbus, 1964). Richard Hofstadter, in *The Age of Reform* (New York, 1955), and Otis L. Graham, Jr., in *An Encore for Reform: The Old Progressives and the New Deal* (New York, 1967), challenged this thesis, but it was developed in a new way in the 1960's by J. Joseph Huthmacher. See his "Urban Liberalism and the Age of Reform," *Mississippi Valley Historical Review,* 49 (1962), 231–241; "Charles Evans Hughes and Charles Francis Murphy: The Metamorphosis of Progressivism," *New York History,* 46 (1965), 25–40, and *Senator Robert F. Wagner and the Rise of Urban Liberalism* (New York, 1968).

On the New Deal's debts to attitudes and activities of World War I, the 1920's, and the Hoover years, see, in addition to Chambers, Gerald D. Nash, "Experiments in Industrial Mobilization: WIB and NRA," *Mid-America,* 45 (1963), 158–174; Leuchtenburg, "The New Deal and the Analogue of War," in Braeman, *Twentieth-Century America;* Arthur S. Link, "What Happened to the Progressive Movement in the 1920's?" *American Historical Review,* 64 (1959), 833–851; David A. Shannon, *Between the Wars: America, 1919–1941* (Boston, 1965); Donald C. Swain, *Federal Conservation Policy, 1921–1933* (Berkeley and Los Angeles, 1963); Swain, *Wilderness Defender: Horace M. Albright and Conservation* (Chicago, 1970); Gilbert C. Fite, *George N. Peek and the Fight for Farm Parity* (Norman, 1954); James H. Shideler, *Farm Crisis, 1919–1923* (Berkeley and Los Angeles, 1957); William D. Rowley, *M. L. Wilson and the Campaign for the Domestic Allotment Plan* (Lincoln, 1970); Howard Zinn, *LaGuardia in Congress* (Ithaca, 1959);

Harris Gaylord Warren, *Herbert Hoover and the Great Depression* (New York, 1959) ; Albert U. Romasco, *The Poverty of Abundance: Hoover, the Nation, the Depression* (New York, 1965) ; and Jordan A. Schwarz, *The Interregnum of Despair: Hoover, Congress, and the Depression* (Urbana, 1970) . On the New Deal's relations with an even larger tradition involving the rejection of laissez faire see Robert A. Lively, "The American System: A Review Article," *Business History Review*, 29 (1955) , 81–95; Sidney Fine, *Laissez Faire and the General-Welfare State: A Study of Conflict in American Thought, 1865–1901* (Ann Arbor, 1956) ; and Gerald D. Nash, "Industry and the Federal Government: 1850–1933," *Current History*, 48 (1965) .

The change in Hacker's interpretation has been discussed in part in John F. Gerstung, "Louis M. Hacker's Reappraisal of Recent History," *Historian*, 12 (1950) , 140–166. Important illustrations of Hacker's development, other than those reprinted here, are his *A Short History of the New Deal* (New York, 1934) , *The Triumph of American Capitalism* (New York, 1940) , and *The Shaping of the American Tradition* (New York, 1947) . Hofstadter also illustrated the decline of the left in the historical profession in the postwar period. Compare his essay on Roosevelt in *The American Political Tradition and the Men Who Made It* (New York, 1948) with his interpretation of the New Deal in *The Age of Reform*. The most substantial interpretation of the New Deal from the right is Edgar Eugene Robinson's hostile appraisal, *The Roosevelt Leadership, 1933–1945*, (Philadelphia, 1955) . Robinson sees the New Deal as a revolution, as does Mario Einaudi, *The Roosevelt Revolution* (New York, 1959) . Einaudi, however, like Degler, has a positive appraisal of the "revolution."

On the polling of the opinions of historians see Arthur M. Schlesinger, "Rating the Presidents," *Paths to the Present* (Boston, 1964) and Gary M. Maranell, "The Evaluation of Presidents: An Extension of the Schlesinger Polls," *Journal of American History*, 57 (1970) , 104–113. On the dominant assumptions of the historical profession in the late 1950's and early 1960's see Thomas A. Bailey, *Presidential Greatness: The Image and the*

Man from George Washington to the Present (New York, 1966) , Chapter 3; and Robert Allen Skotheim, ed., *The Historian and the Climate of Opinion* (Reading, 1969) .

Irwin Unger discusses the rise of the New Left in "The 'New Left' and American History: Some Recent Trends in United States Historiography," *American Historical Review*, 72 (1967) , 1237–1263. One of the major early figures in this movement was William Appleman Williams, who developed his interpretation of the New Deal in *The Contours of American History* (Cleveland and New York, 1961) , but the New Left interpretation of the New Deal first became prominent in the historical profession with the publication of two essays by Howard Zinn in 1966 and 1967, his "Introduction" to *New Deal Thought* (Indianapolis, 1966) , a collection of essays, and "The Grateful Society," *Columbia University Forum*, 10 (1967) , 28–32. Paul K. Conkin developed a somewhat similar interpretation much more fully in *The New Deal* (New York, 1967) . On New Deal historiography just before the emergence of the New Left, see Richard S. Kirkendall, "The New Deal as Watershed: The Recent Literature," *Journal of American History*, 54 (1968) , 839–852. For a larger survey of the literature that includes the New Left and an appraisal of it, see Alfred B. Rollins, Jr., "Was There Really a Man Named Roosevelt?" in George Athan Billias and Gerald N. Grob, *American History: Retrospect and Prospect* (New York, 1971) . The New Left did not shatter Leuchtenburg's or Degler's confidence in their interpretations. See Leuchtenburg in John A. Garraty, ed., *Interpreting American History: Conversations with Historians* (2 vols., New York, 1970) , Vol. II, pp. 187, 192; Degler, *Out of Our Past*, rev. ed., 1970, pp. 411, 508; and Degler, ed., *The New Deal* (Chicago, 1970) . For a larger appraisal of the New Left interpretation, see Otis L. Graham, Jr., ed., *The New Deal: The Critical Issues* (Boston, 1971) . Graham agrees with the New Left's appraisal of the New Deal's accomplishments but rejects the New Left's explanation; Graham emphasizes the difficulties in the situation, not the ideological weaknesses of the New Dealers.